PETE EVANS

PALEO EVERY DAY

120 DELICIOUS & NOURISHING RECIPES FOR ENERGY AND GOOD HEALTH

MACMILLAN

CONTENTS

HELLO!

If we live to the age of 75 we get to eat around 75,000 meals in our lifetime. I am aiming to live to 125, so that means a lot more meals! I want all of them to be delicious, for sure, but I also want them to give me the good health I desire to take me into my older years.

As a chef, I have personally cooked more than one million meals over the past 25 years. Increasingly, in recent years, I've found myself wanting to translate that hands-on experience into creating dishes that tick all the boxes on a nutritional level. I have always been interested in health and wellbeing, and I have just completed a course on nutrition. I am now a qualified health coach with the authority to speak on the topic of healthy eating. There is so much misleading information out there, and having children and a beautiful partner, Nicola, has reaffirmed that my mission is to help people better understand their own bodies and eat healthy, nurturing meals. I can honestly say that, at the age of 40, I have never felt better in my life than I do now: both emotionally and physically.

This is not a diet book. It's not about strict rules and rigid labels. My main aim is to share with you some of my favourite recipes – recipes that reflect the way I now cook at home for my family and friends. It just happens that the way I cook these days takes a back-to-basics or 'paleo approach', inspired by how humans were originally (and remain) designed to eat.

Eating paleo-style simply means eating the way our ancestors did, before humans began farming and processing food. Our ancestors lived on nutrient-dense vegetables, fruit, nuts, seeds, fish, shellfish, poultry and game – none of the highly processed and refined foods, laden with sugar and starch, that form the bulk of Western diets today. Processed, sugary foods require different metabolic processes than those our bodies were designed for 10,000 years ago. Our genes remain the same, but our food and our waistlines are vastly different.

Although I favour a paleo approach, I'm well aware that there's no one diet that's perfect for everybody. The foods that make you feel vibrant and give you optimum health may cause your neighbour to feel sluggish and gain weight. And to confuse matters more, your body's needs might change from season to season and year to year, which is why it's so important to seek your own answers. Trust what your digestion and metabolism can handle. Use your nutritional intuition. If anything feels too restrictive then take a more moderate approach – you cannot fail in attempting to become healthier.

Personally, my own body works best with a paleo-inspired diet, free of dairy, yeast, wheat, gluten, grains, sugar and anything processed. You might now be asking yourself, 'what on earth does that leave you with?' You'll find the answer to that question in the recipes that follow; they are nutritious, delicious and you definitely won't feel like you're missing out on anything!

I cover quite a few topics in this book. My intention is to give you the information and tools to make your own informed decisions, and discover what truly nourishes your body and ultimately allows you to be the best you can be. Try keeping a journal, writing down what you eat and how you feel, not only afterwards, but a couple of hours later too. This is one of the best ways to figure out what works for your body.

Having healthy, happy relationships, enjoying some form of exercise, and having a rewarding job or career may be even more beneficial than diet for achieving optimum health. You can eat all the leafy greens in the world, but if you're unhappy at home or work, you may never be free of ill health or possibly even disease. Start doing the activities or sports that you love to do, whether that's taking the dog for a run or walking barefoot on the beach. I surf because I love the connection with the ocean's power. My gorgeous mum, Joy, linedances twice a week with her senior citizens group, and if she misses a week I can see the difference in her energy levels instantly.

I am a firm believer that one of the keys to better health is to eat slowly and in a stress-free environment. When I'm at work I will often find a place to eat that is outdoors and free from distraction, so I can fully focus on the meal I am eating. Time around the dinner table with my family is a true pleasure for me, and making it last is beneficial in more ways than one. Numerous studies have shown that when we are distracted, we over-eat and eat too fast, which can have damaging effects on our health. The biggest use of energy in our bodies is the break-down and digestion of food, so the more we slow down, chew our food and really savour it, the more energy we'll have for other things.

It goes without saying that I am all for cooking your own meals. This way, you know exactly what you are eating, there aren't any hidden surprises and you can be proud of the food that you create. I very rarely eat out, I pack my own food for work or when I travel on a plane (well, actually, Nic usually does that), and I love to make breakfast, lunch and dinner every day at home. I'm into freezing soups and stocks for use later on and eating leftovers for breakfast the next day. We have very little, if any, food wastage in our household, which can only be a good thing.

So what exactly should we eat? As I've said, there are no hard and fast rules – it's all about finding what works best for you and your family – but here are some tips to get you going.

- **Go organic.** Organic produce means produce that is free from chemicals, pesticides and other contaminants. I know it isn't always as readily available or as affordable as the alternative, but it tastes better and is better for you. Beware of sneaky marketing tricks, though: many food companies have discovered that slapping words like 'organic' or 'natural' on their labels gives them a greater chance of sales. Look for labels such as the 'Australian Certified Organic' or 'USDA Organic' logos for the real deal. But don't beat yourself up if what you're after isn't available and you have to choose the non-organic alternative – just do your best with the budget you have and with the resources available to you.

- **Know where your food comes from.** There's a lot of wisdom to that old adage 'you are what you eat'. The more nutrients in the produce you consume the more energy and health you will radiate. If you are eating highly processed food and too much protein from animals that have been carelessly raised in stressful environments on foods they weren't designed to eat, then guess what? You, too, will feel stressed and health problems will eventually start to arise. Start searching out local growers markets and community gardens, find online providers that supply grass-fed meats and visit your fish markets and only buy sustainable wild caught seafood.

- **Watch your meat-to-veggie ratio.** I try and limit my protein intake to between 50 and 100 grams per meal per person, and fill the rest of the plate with vegetables.

- **Hydrate, hydrate, hydrate.** Aim to drink at least 2 litres of filtered water per day. I consume about 3 to 4 litres per day, including a litre upon waking every day, which I drink over a 15-minute period to rehydrate my body.

- **Talk to the experts.** Farmers and growers markets are fun to visit and you can learn so much by talking to the growers. I always ask them for their own recipes; if anyone knows what to do with the produce, it's got to be the people that grow it.

- **Eat seasonally.** Always try to eat foods that are in season: there is a bountiful supply that needs to be sold, so the prices are generally cheaper.

- **Go for quality, not quantity.** The healthiest meals are those that are high in quality fat, moderate in animal protein and low in sugar and starches. Forget calorie-counting and instead focus on portion control.

- **Remember that fats aren't all bad.** Consume some saturated fats such as extra-virgin coconut oil and clarified butter (if your body can tolerate dairy). Olive, avocado and macadamia oils are excellent for salads and to drizzle over food, but not for cooking as they become oxidised when heated. Oxidation causes free radicals in the body, which can speed up the ageing processes. Beef, duck and pork fat are okay if they come from organic sources.

- **Go veggie crazy.** Eat unlimited amounts of non-starchy vegetables, such as green vegetables, lettuce, cauliflower, broccoli, green beans and peppers – either raw or cooked. Eat a moderate amount of sweet potatoes and yams, too, as they're a great source of fibre and slow-releasing carbohydrates.

- **Treat yourself.** Enjoy low to moderate amounts of fruit and nuts. Berries, apples and pears are lower in sugar than mangoes and other tropical fruits. Berries are antioxidant-rich and nuts are full of essential fatty acids.

- **Experiment.** Try cutting out all cereal grains and legumes from your diet. This includes wheat, rye, barley, oats, corn, brown rice, soy (unless fermented, as in miso, tamari or natto), peanuts, kidney beans, pinto beans and black-eyed peas. If you do add some grains or legumes, I suggest soaking or sprouting them to break down the enzymes and help digestion.

- **Spice it up.** Use plenty of spices and herbs to enhance your meals. Not only do they taste delicious, they are jam-packed with health benefits.

- **Achieve balance.** Food and diet is one thing, but to obtain a balanced, healthy life you need to find harmony in everything from your relationships to your job.

- **Remove temptation.** Get rid of all the foods in your fridge, freezer and pantry that you know are not helping you to achieve your health goals. You know what they are, so go on, be strong and throw them away! You will feel so much better and so empowered by removing them from your home.

- **Share your journey.** Make sure that you're open, proud and honest with your family and friends about your quest for better health. Ask them for support in your decision, so that they can stand by you and assist you on your way.

A paleo-inspired diet is not about restrictions. Think of it as adding so much good into your diet that you forget, or are no longer hungry for, the bad. Eating quality proteins like grass-fed beef and wild-caught fish, as well as eggs, nuts, seeds and healthy fats like coconut oil, ghee, olive and nut oils gives you an unbeatable satiated feeling. When you eat like this, you simply don't have room for the sugar and starches found in processed cereals, packaged breads, pastas, lollies, 'healthy' muesli bars, sugary yoghurts and energy drinks. I can honestly say I've never looked back and have never felt better!

The recipes in this book reflect what works for me and for my family, but I encourage you to experiment with them and create your own dishes. I truly believe that food is a celebration, something that brings people together. My daughters, who are now 7 and 8, always set the table and help with the preparation of our meals, and then we all sit down together and take the time to enjoy the food and each other's company. I hope this book inspires you to get into the kitchen and not only create delicious meals, but to truly take pride in nourishing yourself, your family and your friends.

Cheers.

Pete

www.peteevanschef.com
Cook with Love and Laughter!

Due to its high sugar content, I view fruit as a treat to have from time to time. The fruit I have at home is usually organic, and often includes fresh or frozen berries, watermelon, green apples and bananas (I keep them in the freezer to add to smoothies or for making dairy-free ice cream). This simple dish is ideal on a hot summer's day as it's truly refreshing and light. If you don't have a melon baller, simply cut the watermelon into small pieces.

WATERMELON, FIG, DATE AND PISTACHIO SALAD

500 g watermelon balls

6 medjool dates, pitted and sliced into thin slivers

¼ teaspoon fine sea salt

1 tablespoon lime juice

4 fresh figs, cut into quarters

45 g shelled pistachio nuts, toasted and roughly chopped

1 teaspoon black chia seeds

few drops of rosewater

Place the watermelon and dates in a large bowl.

Stir the salt into the lime juice in a small bowl, then drizzle over the salad and toss well. Gently toss through the figs. Refrigerate until well chilled.

Serve sprinkled with the pistachio nuts, chia seeds and rosewater.

SERVES 4

NOTE

Our bodies can't differentiate between natural and processed sugars, so whether we eat high-fructose fruit like bananas, or sucrose-laden cakes and biscuits, the sugars still cause insulin spikes, weight gain and other problems. Although fruit sugar is broken down more slowly by the body, causing less of a sugar spike, excess consumption may still lead to weight gain or, even worse, liver problems. Sadly, most fruit these days has been genetically engineered to be super sweet and oversized. The key is to source organic, seasonal fruit and only eat it in moderate amounts.

I eat chia seed puddings regularly – sometimes for breakfast, sometimes as a snack and sometimes as dessert. Chia seeds are absolutely packed with goodies, including omega-3 fatty acids, calcium, potassium, vitamin C and antioxidants. These puddings are really simple to make and the flavour combinations are endless. As the seasons change, you can experiment with different fruits, and instead of coconut cream, try using coconut water, nut milks (page 233), vegetable and fruit juices, or even teas.

CHIA SEED PUDDINGS

1 young coconut*

125 ml coconut cream or coconut milk

50 g chia seeds*

3 tablespoons honey, or to taste

your choice of flavouring (see ideas below)

* See Glossary

Open the coconut by cutting a circular hole in the top. Pour the coconut water into a jug (you should get about 250 ml). Use a spoon to scoop the meat out of the coconut (you should get about 120 g).

Place the coconut flesh in a food processor with 125 ml of the coconut water and process until you have a smooth, thick puree.

Pour into a bowl, add the coconut cream or milk, chia seeds and honey and mix well. Stir through your choice of flavouring (see ideas below). Transfer the mixture to small glasses and refrigerate for at least 2 hours before serving.

SERVES 2–4 (DEPENDING ON HOW HUNGRY YOU ARE!)

FLAVOUR VARIATIONS

Banana, spirulina and toasted pistachio
Add 2 mashed bananas and 1 teaspoon of spirulina to the chia pudding recipe above. Serve with sliced banana, chopped, toasted pistachio nuts and a drizzle of honey.

Mixed berry and sunflower seed
Place 150 g of fresh or frozen mixed berries and 1 tablespoon of honey in a blender or food processor and blend until smooth. Pass through a sieve to remove the seeds and set aside. Fold another 100 g of mixed berries into the chia pudding recipe above. To serve, pour the puree over the pudding, arrange some extra berries on top and sprinkle with sunflower seeds.

Vanilla bean, macadamia and toasted coconut
Mix the seeds from 1 vanilla bean and 50 g chopped, toasted macadamia nuts into the chia pudding recipe above. Serve with toasted coconut shavings, extra chopped, toasted macadamia nuts and a drizzle of honey.

Mixed berry and sunflower seed

Banana, spirulina and
toasted pistachio

Vanilla bean, macadamia and
toasted coconut

My girlfriend, Nic, and I love experimenting with new recipes, and the kids are our best critics as they're always brutally honest. Nic certainly has a knack for the pastry side of the kitchen; she never follows recipes, but instead creates her own. My daughters requested pancakes recently and Nic whipped up these almond and berry ones. They're a delicious treat for a big family breakfast. Play around with different seasonal fruits, or add carob and nuts to create your own personal touch.

ALMOND AND BERRY PANCAKES

4 eggs

120 ml almond milk (or any other milk you like)

½ teaspoon natural vanilla extract

2 tablespoons honey, plus extra to serve

100 g ground almonds

2 teaspoons baking powder

1½ tablespoons coconut flour

pinch of sea salt

pinch of ground cinnamon

ghee or coconut oil, for cooking, plus extra coconut oil to serve

160 g fresh berries

lemon juice, to serve

fresh fruit, to serve

In a small bowl, whisk the eggs for about 2 minutes, or until frothy. Mix in the milk, vanilla and honey.

Combine the ground almonds, baking powder, coconut flour, salt and cinnamon in a bowl.

Add the egg mixture to the dry ingredients and mix well.

Grease a large frying pan with a little ghee or coconut oil and place over medium heat. Ladle a few tablespoons of batter into the pan for each pancake and spread out slightly with the back of a spoon. The pancakes should be 5–6 cm in diameter and fairly thick. Cook for a few minutes on each side, until the tops dry out slightly and the bottoms start to brown. Flip and cook for an additional 2–3 minutes.

Serve hot topped with fresh berries, coconut oil, honey, a squeeze of lemon juice and fresh fruit.

SERVES 2

TIPS

Ghee is clarified butter and it can be found at Indian food stores and some supermarkets.

You can top these pancakes with whatever fruit you like – try sliced nectarines, bananas or pears.

Keep the pancakes small in size, and don't get distracted while cooking them as they can burn easily.

Gluten intolerance is becoming so prevalent these days, especially in children.
My eldest daughter, Chilli, loves her muesli, but has a gluten and wheat intolerance.
Unfortunately, many of the gluten-free muesli options are much too high in sugar.
So my girlfriend, Nic, created this healthy mix of nuts and seeds and it has become
Chilli's favourite. You will need to start this recipe two days in advance.

CHILLI'S MUESLI

160 g almonds

160 g macadamia nuts

100 g buckwheat*

75 g sunflower seeds

75 g pumpkin seeds

40 g sesame seeds

2 tablespoons ground flaxseeds
or chia seeds*

120 g goji berries*

2 pink lady apples, peeled, cored
and roughly chopped

80 ml coconut oil

1 tablespoon ground cinnamon

1 tablespoon vanilla powder
(or 1 teaspoon vanilla extract)

1 tablespoon licorice root powder*

1 teaspoon ground ginger

pinch of sea salt

honey, to taste (optional)

65 g shredded coconut

Nut Milk (page 233) or coconut
milk, to serve

fresh blueberries and raspberries,
to serve

* *See Glossary*

Place the nuts, buckwheat and seeds in a large bowl. Cover with room-temperature water and soak for 7 hours. Also place the goji berries in a small bowl, add just enough water to cover and soak overnight.

The following day, preheat the oven to 50°C, or as low as it will go. Line a large tray with baking paper.

Drain the nuts, buckwheat and seeds and rinse well. Dry thoroughly using a clean tea towel or paper towel and process in a food processor. It's up to you how long you process them for, depending on whether you prefer a chunky or fine muesli. Transfer the nuts, buckwheat and seeds to a bowl and rinse the food processor.

Drain the goji berries and place in the food processor. Add the apple, coconut oil, cinnamon, vanilla powder, licorice root powder, ginger, salt and honey (if using) and process to a fine puree.

Combine the two mixtures in a large bowl and stir well. Spread out on the prepared tray and place in the oven for 6–8 hours, or until you reach your desired level of crunch. Carefully give your muesli a light toss every couple of hours.

Remove the muesli from the oven and allow to cool before breaking it into bite-sized pieces. Combine with the shredded coconut and store in an airtight glass container for up to 4 weeks.

Serve with nut or coconut milk and a sprinkling of blueberries and raspberries.

SERVES 6

This porridge is a fabulous way to start the day. Berries are packed full of antioxidants, vitamins and other nutrients, while quinoa has loads of protein. There are now a number of quinoa producers in Tasmania, so look out for Australian-grown quinoa when you are buying it.

QUINOA AND BERRY PORRIDGE

300 g quinoa*, rinsed

500 ml coconut milk (or any other milk you like)

2 teaspoons natural vanilla extract

1 teaspoon ground cinnamon

160 g macadamia nuts, roughly chopped

60 g goji berries*

150 g blueberries (fresh or frozen)

2 tablespoons coconut flakes, to serve

honey, to serve (optional)

extra coconut milk, to serve (optional)

* *See Glossary*

Place the quinoa in a saucepan with the coconut milk and vanilla. Bring to a simmer over medium heat. Reduce the heat, cover and simmer for 20 minutes, or until the quinoa is light and fluffy.

Fluff the quinoa with a fork and allow it to cool a little before stirring through the cinnamon, macadamia nuts and goji berries.

Spoon into bowls and scatter over blueberries and coconut flakes. Add a drizzle of honey (if using) and extra coconut milk, if desired.

SERVES 4

TIP

You can personalise this recipe by topping the porridge with any fresh or dried fruit, seeds or nuts just before serving. Your choices are endless, but if you need some help getting started, try banana, kiwifruit, apple, stone fruit, chia seeds, toasted shredded coconut or young coconut flesh.

Try adding some grated beetroot to your sprouted seed bread dough before baking. Yum!

This is without a doubt the best bread I've ever eaten! It is free from gluten, wheat, sugar, soy, egg and grain, yet is high in protein and riboflavin, and is alkaline-forming too. My good mate Pete Melov has been making this bread for the last decade and has kindly shared his recipe. Pete activates the seeds prior to making the bread so that they are easier to digest and their nutrients are easier to absorb. This recipe is for a sprouted quinoa and chia loaf but Pete makes about 20 different loaves, from a turmeric millet loaf to loaves that have slowly simmered lamb shank meat baked into them or are loaded with vegetables and herbs. Slice and toast this bread to serve. You will need to start this recipe the day before.

PETE'S SPROUTED SEED BREAD

360 g buckwheat*

180 g black quinoa* or sorghum

180 g cup hulled millet*

coconut oil, for greasing

70 g chia seeds*

1 tablespoon sea salt

1 tablespoon pau d'arco powder*

1 teaspoon maca powder*

1 tablespoon slippery elm powder*

avocado, to serve

beetroot hummus (for a recipe, see page 186), to serve

* See Glossary

Place the buckwheat, quinoa and millet in a large bowl, add enough water to cover by 5 cm and soak overnight. Drain and set aside.

Preheat the oven to 180°C. Grease a 22 cm × 12 cm loaf tin with coconut oil and line the base and sides with baking paper.

Pour 250 ml of water into a food processor – it's essential to use a food processor, not a blender, otherwise the mix will be too fine and your loaf will end up more like a brick than bread. Slowly add the chia seeds and pulse. Add all the other ingredients and continue to pulse until the dough has a porridge-like consistency (not like a normal bread dough!). You may need to add more chia seeds if the dough is too thin, or a little more water if the dough is too thick.

Pour the dough into the prepared tin and bake for 2½ hours, or until a skewer inserted in the centre of the loaf comes out clean. (You will need to do the skewer test as this bread is a lot denser than regular bread and won't sound hollow when you tap it.)

Remove the loaf from the tin and allow to cool on a cooling rack. Serve lightly toasted and slathered with avocado and beetroot hummus. It is also fabulous with cultured vegetables and chicken liver pâté (page 144), or as a side for a salad, stew or curry. You can store this bread at room temperature for 2 days, in the refrigerator for up to 5 days, or in the freezer for 3 months.

SERVES 6

TIPS

Sorghum is a gluten-free grain and is available from health food stores.

You can use other herbs and spices in this recipe – try turmeric, wattle seed, sage, rosemary or cumin – to make it even more interesting. Simply add any extra herbs and spices to the food processor with all of the other ingredients.

I have always been fascinated by the flavours of Central and South America: the salsas, guacamole, coriander, ceviches, the marinades for meat dishes ... the list goes on. I eat an avocado almost every day when they're in season because they're packed full of nutrients, including oleic acid and omega-3 fatty acids. When you team avocado with a wonderful protein like prawns, you've got a meal that ticks all the boxes for a tasty, healthy meal. Enjoy this Mexican breakfast dish that's fun to make and really excites the tastebuds.

MEXICAN FRITTATA with PRAWNS AND AVOCADO SALSA

8 large eggs

sea salt and freshly ground black pepper

1 handful of coriander leaves, finely chopped

finely grated zest of 1 lemon

juice of ¼ lemon

200 g shelled and deveined raw prawns

1 tablespoon coconut oil

dried chilli flakes, to serve

1 handful of rocket, to serve

AVOCADO SALSA

2 avocados, diced

2 tomatoes, diced

¼ red onion, diced

1 garlic clove, finely chopped

1 large handful of coriander leaves, roughly chopped

juice of 2 limes

1 tablespoon extra-virgin olive oil

2 jalapeno chillies, halved, seeded and very thinly sliced

Preheat the oven to 220°C.

In a bowl, whisk the eggs with a pinch of salt and pepper, then add the coriander, lemon zest and juice. Roughly chop the prawns and add to the bowl.

In a small ovenproof frying pan, melt the coconut oil over medium heat and add the egg mixture. Slowly move a spoon around the eggs for about a minute, then put the pan in the oven for 4–5 minutes, or until the eggs are lightly golden. The frittata will rise slightly and have a delicious lightness to it. (You often get frittata that is very firm, but I'd rather have it in a hot oven for a shorter amount of time, so there's a little colour on top and the middle is cooked but not absolutely set.)

Meanwhile, mix the avocado salsa ingredients in a bowl.

Once the frittata is cooked, remove from the oven and slide onto a board or plate. To serve, top with the avocado salsa, chilli flakes and rocket.

SERVES 4

I love everything about dukkah: the aroma, the texture, the taste and even the look of it. In fact, just hearing the word 'dukkah' gets my tastebuds buzzing. Dukkah is a traditional Egyptian side dish made from dry roasted spices, nuts and seeds. It works well with just about anything, but one of my favourite ways to serve it is with softly cooked, runny-yolked eggs and green tahini. You can often find green tahini in delis and health food shops, but it's also really easy to make your own using your favourite herbs. If you don't have time to make the green tahini, you can just use regular unhulled tahini

EGGS WITH DUKKAH, GREEN TAHINI AND CULTURED BEETROOT

8 eggs, at room temperature

160 g dukkah (for a recipe, see page 190)

olive oil, for brushing

125 ml Green Tahini (page 246)

4 tablespoons Cultured Beetroot, Apple and Carrot (page 207), to serve

sea salt and freshly ground black pepper

Place the eggs in a saucepan and add enough cold water to cover them by 1 cm. Place over medium heat and bring to the boil. Reduce the heat and simmer for 3–4 minutes, depending on how runny you like your yolks. If you prefer your eggs hard-boiled, simmer for 6–7 minutes. Drain the eggs, run them under cold water to cool, then peel.

Place the dukkah in a small bowl. Brush the eggs with olive oil and roll them in the dukkah to form a crust. If you would like a thicker crust, lightly brush the eggs with olive oil again and roll them in the dukkah once more. Gently press the dukkah with the palm of your hands to create a nice, even coating.

Spread some green tahini on each plate and pop 2 eggs on top. Serve with a spoonful each of cultured beetroot, apple and carrot and season with salt and pepper.

SERVES 4

Sardines have to be one of my favourite fish; however, this wasn't always the case. I can still remember how freaked out I was when my Dad opened a can and spread the contents on his toasted white bread. I just couldn't understand how he wasn't as disgusted as I was. But I grew up and my palate evolved to enjoy this nutritionally dense fish. The reason I love sardines, apart from the fact that they're delicious and affordable, is that they're a great source of omega-3 fatty acids, calcium and vitamin D. In this dish I have teamed the sardines with eggs and an Israeli paprika and tomato sauce – a very satisfying breakfast.

BAKED EGGS WITH SARDINES

4 green banana peppers

4 garlic cloves, finely chopped

2–3 teaspoons smoked paprika

3 tablespoons coconut oil

12 large tomatoes, roughly chopped

sea salt and freshly ground black pepper

8 eggs

2 tablespoons chopped coriander leaves

8 sardines, butterflied, heads and bones removed

2 tablespoons chermoula (for a recipe, see page 246)

Preheat the grill to high. Grill the banana peppers (or cook over a flame) until their skin is blackened and blistered. Put in a plastic bag or cover with a tea towel and set aside to sweat. When cool, peel off the blackened skin, remove the seeds and finely slice the flesh.

Preheat the oven to 180°C.

To make the paprika and tomato sauce, combine the garlic, paprika, oil and tomatoes in a small saucepan over medium–low heat, season and bring to the boil. Cover, reduce the heat and simmer for 10 minutes, or until the tomato has softened and the sauce has thickened. Adjust the seasoning to taste and transfer to 4 small ovenproof dishes or ramekins (if you don't have 4 small dishes, use 1 large ovenproof dish instead).

Make 2 wells in the sauce in each dish and crack an egg into each one. Sprinkle over the coriander and pepper strips, then add 2 sardines to each dish. Season with more salt and pepper and bake for 5 minutes, or until the eggs and sardines are just cooked. Pull out of the oven, top with some chermoula and serve.

SERVES 4

TIP

We're fortunate in Australia to have access to fresh sardines pretty much all year round, but if you can't find any, there are some good-quality frozen and canned varieties available.

One of my favourite ways to start the day in the cooler months is with a soup. Hands down, my favourite is miso, not only for its health benefits, but because it tastes so good and is so easy to prepare. Miso is a delicious fermented paste (most commonly made from soy beans) that has been eaten in China and Japan for many centuries. Today it is a favourite of health-conscious people in the West because of its many anti-ageing properties. Miso and other fermented foods and drinks help ensure the digestive tract is amply supplied with beneficial bacteria.

MISO SOUP WITH SALMON

½ tablespoon wakame*

¼ small cauliflower head (about 200 g), cut into small florets

¼ daikon*, cut into 1 cm pieces

3 spring onions, finely sliced

16 okra*, roughly chopped

½ bunch of broccolini (about 100 g), roughly chopped

1 sweet potato (about 200 g), chopped and roasted

125 ml miso paste*

200 g salmon fillet, skinned and pin-boned, cut into 5 mm thick pieces

TO SERVE

toasted sesame seeds

sesame oil

dried chilli flakes (optional)

chopped coriander leaves

* See Glossary

Bring 1 litre of water to the boil over medium heat. Add the wakame and simmer for about 20 minutes, or until it has expanded. Add the vegetables and cook for 2–5 minutes, or until just tender.

Add the miso – the best way to do this is to push it through a strainer into the pan, to help distribute it evenly in the water. When the miso is dissolved (about 1–2 minutes – stir if you need to), the soup is ready.

Place some salmon in the base of 4 warm bowls and pour over the soup. To serve, scatter over some sesame seeds and add 1–2 drops of sesame oil, some chilli flakes (if using) and chopped coriander.

SERVES 4

VARIATIONS

Play around with different ingredients based on seasonality and what you have in the fridge. Try other seafood, such as cooked prawns. Bok choy and mushrooms are also great additions, or try it with some kimchi (for a recipe, see page 208) on the side.

STOCKS

Homemade stocks are a staple in our home, not only for the flavour they add to dishes, but also for the many healing minerals and nutrients they contain. I realise that it's tempting to purchase pre-made stocks, but believe me, homemade stocks are much more nutrient-dense and affordable, and taste so much better! I urge you to give it a go. A big batch of stock using leftover chicken, beef or fish bones, or simply veggies, can be used in a host of recipes, or stored in the freezer for future use. We often dedicate one day a week to making a big batch of rich, flavourful stock.

GELATINE

Homemade stock that resembles jelly after being refrigerated is a sign of a really nutritious stock. Stock gelatine has numerous health benefits, from boosting immunity to improving digestion. If your stock isn't gelatinous after being refrigerated, it could be the type of bones you've used or that you've added too much water. Don't despair if your stock lacks the clear gel, it will still taste delicious and be nutritious.

VEGETABLE AND HERB ADDITIONS

You can play around with the flavour of your stock in a number of ways. Chopped vegetables such as onion, garlic, celery, leek or carrot add wonderful flavour dimensions. We tend to add whatever we have in the garden or the fridge, with the exception of foods that will make your stock bitter, like broccoli, turnip, cabbage, brussels sprouts, green pepper, collard greens and mustard greens. Herbs add a lovely flavour and extra medicinal benefits, too. Parsley, rosemary, oregano, thyme, curry leaves, kaffir lime and bay leaves are often used in recipes for stocks. But there are no hard and fast rules as to what you add to your bones. With or without veggies and herbs, your stocks will have a divine flavour.

APPLE CIDER VINEGAR

The addition of apple cider vinegar helps draw more calcium and other minerals out of the bones. I recommend using about 1 tablespoon of apple cider vinegar per litre of water.

BOILING VERSUS SIMMERING

I find both methods work just fine, but if you're after a clear consistency, then your best bet is to simmer your stock.

ROASTING BONES

Roasting bones prior to boiling gives stock a rich flavour and dark colour. This step is optional and I tend to do this only when making stocks for soups due to the intense flavour it adds.

STORAGE

The best way to store stock is to freeze it, especially if you boil the stock down to a dense consistency. I like to freeze small portions to easily thaw and add to our dishes.

TYPES OF BONE

Any bones you have available will make good stock. If you are shopping solely for soup bones, don't be afraid to step outside your comfort zone – calf's foot, chicken feet and fish heads are particularly gelatinous and flavoursome ingredients. Also, you're going to get many more health benefits from organic, free-range, grass-fed and humanely raised poultry and meat.

METHOD

As I said, there are no hard and fast rules for making stock, so choose whatever works for you and adapt it to suit your budget and schedule. This is what works for me, but feel free to create your own method.

- Brown the bones in the oven if you have time. (Do this if you're making stock for soups as it adds more flavour.)

- Place the bones in a stockpot or large saucepan.

- Add vegetables and herbs. (I usually use celery, carrot, onion, ginger, turmeric, licorice root, garlic, chilli and coriander roots.)

- Cover the bones, vegetables and herbs with water. Set the water level about 3 cm above the bones.

- Add the apple cider vinegar.

- Cover the pan, with the lid slightly ajar, place over low heat and bring to a simmer.

- Keep the lid slightly ajar as the stock warms up to avoid boiling. Or, if you wish it to boil, make sure you have enough liquid to ensure you're not left with burnt bones.

- Simmer the stock for 2–8 hours. (Fish and vegetable stocks process more quickly; chicken and beef stocks take much longer.)

- Strain the stock and it's ready to use. Store any leftovers in an airtight container in the freezer or fridge.

- If you wish, you can add water to the bones again and make a second batch of stock. Second-time-round stocks are good for cooking sprouted quinoa and buckwheat due to their milder flavour.

VEGETABLE STOCK

1 tablespoon coconut oil

1 onion, roughly chopped

2 large carrots, roughly chopped

2 parsnips, roughly chopped

1 celery stalk, roughly chopped

½ large bunch of Swiss chard (about 600 g)

several thyme sprigs

several flat-leaf parsley stalks

1 dried bay leaf

In a stockpot or large saucepan, melt the coconut oil over medium–high heat. Add the onion and cook, stirring, for about 8 minutes, or until caramelised. Add the carrot, parsnip and celery and cook for about 15 minutes, or until tender.

Wash and drain the Swiss chard thoroughly and chop into 2.5 cm pieces. Add to the pot, along with 4 litres of water and the thyme, parsley and bay leaf. Bring to the boil, reduce the heat to low, cover and simmer for about 1 hour, or until the stock is highly flavoured.

Remove the stock from the heat and strain through a fine sieve, pressing on the vegetables to extract all their juices. Pour into storage containers for the fridge or freezer. Discard the vegetables, unless you are keeping them to use in soup or coconut dressing (page 255).

The stock can be refrigerated for 3–4 days or frozen for up to 3 months.

MAKES ABOUT 3½ LITRES

FISH STOCK

2 tablespoons coconut oil

2 onions, roughly chopped

1 carrot, roughly chopped

125 ml dry white wine or vermouth (optional)

3–4 whole, non-oily fish carcasses (including heads), such as snapper, barramundi or sole

3 tablespoons apple cider vinegar*

several thyme sprigs

several flat-leaf parsley stalks

1 dried bay leaf

See Glossary

Melt the oil in a stockpot or large saucepan over medium–low heat. Add the vegetables and cook very gently for about 30 minutes, or until soft. Pour in the wine or vermouth (if using) and bring to the boil. Add the fish carcasses and cover with 3 litres of cold water. Stir in the vinegar and bring to the boil, skimming off the scum and impurities as they rise to the top.

Tie the herbs together with kitchen string and add to the pan. Reduce the heat to low, cover and simmer for at least 2 hours.

Remove the carcasses with tongs or a slotted spoon and strain the liquid into storage containers for the fridge or freezer. Chill well in the fridge and remove any congealed fat before transferring to the freezer for long-term storage. The stock will keep for 2–3 days in the fridge or 2 months in the freezer.

MAKES ABOUT 2 ½ LITRES

SOUPS

CHICKEN STOCK

1–1.5 kg bony chicken parts, such as
necks, backs, breastbones and wings

2–4 chicken feet (optional)

2 tablespoons apple cider vinegar*

1 large onion, roughly chopped

2 carrots, roughly chopped

3 celery stalks, roughly chopped

2 leeks, white part only, rinsed and
roughly chopped

1 garlic bulb, cut in half lengthways

1 tablespoon black peppercorns,
lightly crushed

2 large handfuls of flat-leaf
parsley stalks

See Glossary

Place the chicken pieces and feet (if using) in a stockpot or large saucepan and
add 4 litres of cold water, the vinegar, onion, carrots, celery, leek, garlic and
peppercorns. Allow to stand for 30 minutes to 1 hour.

Place over medium–high heat and bring to the boil, skimming off any scum
that forms on the surface of the liquid. Reduce the heat to low and simmer for
6–8 hours, or until the meat has completely fallen off the bone. The longer
you cook the stock the richer and more flavourful it will be. About 10 minutes
before the stock is ready, add the parsley.

Strain the stock through a fine sieve into a large storage container, cover and
place in the fridge until the fat rises to the top and congeals. Skim off this fat
and reserve the stock in covered containers in the fridge or freezer. The stock
will keep for 3–4 days in the fridge or 2–3 months in the freezer.

MAKES ABOUT 3 1/2 LITRES

SOUPS

BEEF STOCK

2 kg beef knuckle and marrow bones

1 calf's foot, cut into pieces (optional)

3 tablespoons apple cider vinegar*

1.5 kg meaty rib or neck bones

3 onions, roughly chopped

3 carrots, roughly chopped

3 celery stalks, roughly chopped

2 leeks, white part only, rinsed and roughly chopped

several thyme sprigs, tied together

1 teaspoon black peppercorns, crushed

1 garlic bulb, cut in half lengthways

2 large handfuls of flat-leaf parsley stalks

Place the knuckle and marrow bones and calf's foot (if using) in a stockpot or very large saucepan. Add the vinegar and pour in 4 litres of cold water, or enough to cover. Let stand for 1 hour.

Preheat the oven to 175°C.

Meanwhile, place the meaty bones in a roasting tin and roast for 10 minutes, or until well browned. Add to the pan along with the vegetables. Pour the fat out of the roasting tin into a saucepan. Add 1 litre of water, place over high heat and bring to a simmer, stirring with a wooden spoon to loosen any coagulated juices. Add this liquid to the bones and vegetables. Add additional water, if necessary, to cover the bones; but the liquid should come no higher than within 2 cm of the rim of the pan, as the volume expands slightly during cooking.

Bring the stock to the boil, skimming off the scum that rises to the top. Reduce the heat to low and add the thyme, peppercorns and garlic.

Simmer the stock for at least 8 hours. The longer you cook the stock the richer and more flavourful it will be. Just before finishing, add the parsley and simmer for another 10 minutes.

Strain the stock into a large container. Cover and cool in the fridge. Remove the congealed fat that rises to the top. Transfer to smaller airtight containers and place in the fridge or, for long-term storage, the freezer. The stock will keep for 2–4 days in the fridge or up to 3 months in the freezer.

MAKES ABOUT 4 LITRES

SOUPS

I am a big fan of soup. You can create the most wonderful depth of flavour, really highlighting the ingredients you are using, especially vegetables. When carrots are in season and at their best and cheapest, I love to whip up a big pot of this soup. The addition of crispy fried tempeh adds some much-needed texture, and the hint of miso gives it an added umami flavour, making it very addictive. If tempeh is hard to come by, then some leftover roasted chicken or even some prawns make a lovely addition.

CARROT AND PUMPKIN SOUP WITH TEMPEH

3 tablespoons coconut oil

1 kg carrots, finely sliced

450 g pumpkin, diced

1 large onion, finely chopped

4 garlic cloves, smashed

1.3 litres chicken stock (for a recipe, see page 38) or vegetable stock (for a recipe, see page 36)

1 tablespoon finely grated ginger, or more to taste

3 tablespoons white miso paste*, or more to taste

sea salt and freshly ground black pepper

200 g tempeh*, diced

sesame oil, to serve

2 spring onions, very finely sliced, to serve

* See Glossary

Melt 2 tablespoons of the oil in a large saucepan over medium heat. Add the carrots, pumpkin, onion and garlic and sauté, stirring occasionally, for about 10 minutes, or until the onion is translucent. Add the stock and ginger, reduce the heat, cover and simmer, stirring occasionally, for about 30 minutes, or until the carrot is tender.

Puree the soup using a hand-held blender.

Whisk together the miso and 125 ml of the pureed soup in a small bowl. Stir the mixture back into the soup. Taste and season with salt, pepper or additional ginger or miso.

Melt the remaining coconut oil in a frying pan, add the tempeh and cook over medium heat for 2–3 minutes, or until lightly browned. Set aside.

Ladle the soup into bowls and garnish with a drizzle of sesame oil and a small mound of spring onion and tempeh.

SERVES 4

Mustard seeds and curry leaves popping in the bottom of a saucepan creates a delightfully seductive aroma. This soup is a wonderful example of how carefully blended spices can enhance a humble vegetable. If you have never roasted cauliflower before, then I urge you to try, as I reckon this is the best technique for showing off the beautiful flavour of this vegetable. Play around with different spice combinations or, for the best snack, just sprinkle on some cumin and sea salt and roast until golden. The key is to roast it so it is nearly burnt; not black but a beautiful, deep golden brown.

INDIAN SPICED CAULIFLOWER SOUP

4 tablespoons coconut oil

1 cauliflower head, cut into florets (see tip)

1 garlic clove, finely chopped

sea salt

1 tablespoon yellow mustard seeds

10 curry leaves*

3 onions, chopped

¼ teaspoon cayenne pepper

750 ml chicken stock (for a recipe, see page 38) or vegetable stock (for a recipe, see page 36)

1½ teaspoons apple cider vinegar*

freshly ground black pepper

1 small handful of coriander leaves, to serve

toasted cumin seeds, to serve

GARAM MASALA

3 tablespoons coriander seeds

3 tablespoons cumin seeds

5–6 cinnamon sticks, broken into pieces

1 tablespoon cardamom pods

1 tablespoon whole cloves

1 teaspoon fennel seeds

* See Glossary

To make the garam masala, toast the spices and seeds in a small saucepan over medium heat, shaking the pan to move them about, for about 3 minutes, or until dark and fragrant. Set aside to cool.

Grind the spices to a fine powder in a spice grinder or using a mortar and pestle.

Preheat the oven to 200°C.

Melt 2 tablespoons of the coconut oil. On a large baking tray, toss the cauliflower florets and garlic with the melted coconut oil and 1 teaspoon of the garam masala. Sprinkle on a little salt and roast for 25 minutes, or until the cauliflower is golden and the garlic is aromatic. Remove from the oven and set aside.

Heat the remaining coconut oil in a large saucepan over medium–high heat. Add the mustard seeds and curry leaves and cook for 1 minute. Add the onion and cook for 3–4 minutes, or until softened. Add 3 teaspoons of the garam masala, the cayenne pepper, cauliflower and garlic and cook for a few minutes until fragrant. Add the stock and 750 ml of water and bring to the boil. Reduce the heat to low and simmer for 10–15 minutes, or until the cauliflower is really soft. Remove from the heat and blend until smooth. Stir in the vinegar. Taste and add salt and pepper, if necessary.

Ladle the soup into bowls and top with coriander leaves, a sprinkle of toasted cumin seeds and the reserved cauliflower florets, if using (see tip).

SERVES 4

TIPS

The garam masala can be stored in an airtight glass container for up to 3 months. Also, if you'd like the soup with chunks of cauliflower, roast an extra ½ head of cauliflower. Use two-thirds of the cauliflower florets to make the soup and add the remaining roasted cauliflower florets to each bowl before serving.

Top with extra roasted
cauliflower to make this an
even heartier meal.

This is a soup I love to make at home, changing the veggies depending on seasonality and availability. It is a simple soup to digest and is great for breakfast. You could, of course, add some protein; try leftover roasted chicken, braised lamb shanks or oxtail or, for a seafood hit, some prawns or wild salmon.

WARMING VEGETABLE SOUP

2 tablespoons coconut oil

1 large brown onion, chopped

1½ teaspoons sea salt, plus extra to taste

2 garlic cloves, chopped

3 tablespoons chopped ginger, plus more to taste

1 large leek, white and light green parts only, sliced

1 large sweet potato, diced

1 litre chicken stock (for a recipe, see page 38) or vegetable stock (for a recipe, see page 36)

1 bunch of kale (about 400 g), roughly chopped

150 g okra*, cut into 2.5 cm pieces

1 large bunch of Swiss chard, roughly chopped

2–4 teaspoons lemon juice

1 handful of flat-leaf parsley leaves, chopped

freshly ground black pepper

* See Glossary

Melt the oil in a large saucepan over low heat. Add the onion and a sprinkle of salt and cook slowly, stirring now and then, for about 15 minutes, or until the onion is soft and golden. Add the garlic, ginger and leek and cook for a minute. Stir in the sweet potato, stock and 1 teaspoon of the salt and bring to the boil. Reduce the heat, add the kale, okra and Swiss chard and simmer for 15 minutes. You can either puree the soup or leave it chunky.

Stir 2 teaspoons of the lemon juice into the soup. Add the parsley and a few grinds of pepper, then taste. Correct the seasoning with additional salt or lemon juice. Spoon into bowls and serve.

SERVES 6

Marina, David and their daughter Charley are dear friends of mine, and I was fortunate enough to be invited to a wonderful Italian-inspired dinner recently at their home. We started off with the most beautiful soup featuring courgettes from Marina's father's garden. Thanks for sharing the recipe, Marina.

COURGETTE AND PEA SOUP

1 tablespoon coconut oil

2 leeks, white and light green parts only, sliced

3 garlic cloves, chopped

4 large courgettes, diced

200 g fresh or frozen peas

1.3 litres chicken stock (for a recipe, see page 38)

4 thyme sprigs, leaves picked and finely chopped

½ teaspoon freshly grated nutmeg

2 fresh or dried bay leaves

sea salt and freshly ground white pepper

watercress, to serve

chopped, toasted hazelnuts, to serve

Place the coconut oil in a large saucepan and sauté the leek and garlic over medium heat for a few minutes. Add the courgettes and cook for about 5 minutes. Add the peas and 500 ml of the stock and bring to the boil. Reduce the heat and add the thyme, nutmeg, bay leaves and salt and pepper to taste. Cook for another 5 minutes, or until fragrant, then add the remaining stock and simmer for 30 minutes.

Remove the bay leaves and blend until smooth. To serve, top with some watercress and sprinkle with chopped, toasted hazelnuts.

SERVES 6

Every year I spend a week or two in Fiji. I love the people, the surf, the diving, the fishing. The whole feeling of the place is so relaxing, and it's a great way to recharge my batteries. I work alongside the locals and we share recipes and learn from each other. One of my favourites is this soup. It is so simple yet it delivers so much flavour and is a great way to use up the frames and heads of fish so that nothing goes to waste.

FIJIAN FISH SOUP

1 kg fish heads and carcasses, such as cod or snapper

2 teaspoons sea salt

1 large onion, sliced

1 teaspoon black peppercorns, lightly crushed

1 small red chilli, roughly chopped

sea salt and freshly ground black pepper

1 tablespoon lemon juice

600 ml coconut cream

500 g fish fillets (such as snapper, cod or barramundi), cut into 3 cm cubes

finely sliced spring onions, to serve

finely sliced red chilli, to serve

toasted coconut shavings, to serve

Place the fish heads and carcasses in a large saucepan with 1.75 litres of water, the salt, onion, peppercorns and chilli and bring to simmering point. Simmer for about 20 minutes, skimming periodically.

Strain the stock into another large saucepan and adjust the seasoning if necessary. Stir in the lemon juice, coconut cream and fish and reheat over low heat for 4–5 minutes, or until the fish is cooked through. Be careful not to boil as the coconut cream might separate and the fish might overcook.

Ladle the soup into bowls and garnish with spring onions, chilli and coconut shavings.

SERVES 4–5

Chicken soup is so nourishing for the body and soul that nearly every culture features it in one form or another, from Jewish matzo ball soup and Chinese chicken noodle through to Italian *stracciatella* and this Korean ginseng soup. There are a couple of special ingredients in this soup that require a visit to an Asian grocer, but it is well worth it. In the traditional version the chicken is filled with rice. I like to use soaked buckwheat instead as it has more nutritional value and I also prefer the flavour. You will need to start this recipe the day before.

KOREAN GINSENG, CHICKEN AND BUCKWHEAT SOUP

100 g buckwheat*

2 tablespoons pine nuts, toasted

6 garlic cloves, chopped

10 red dates (jujube)*, halved (optional)

5 fresh or dried chestnuts*, peeled and thinly sliced

3 fresh or dried ginseng roots*, sliced lengthways

1 × 1.4 kg chicken

2 litres chicken stock (for a recipe, see page 38)

80 ml tamari*

2 tablespoons finely grated ginger

200 g bok choy, finely chopped

sea salt

2 spring onions, finely chopped

1 teaspoon sesame seeds, toasted

1–2 teaspoons Korean chilli paste (gochujang)* (optional)

2 teaspoons sesame oil

* See Glossary

Place the buckwheat in a bowl, cover with water and soak overnight.

Drain the buckwheat and place in a large bowl. Add the pine nuts, 2 chopped garlic cloves, 2 dates, 2 sliced chestnuts and 1 sliced ginseng root and mix well.

Stuff the cavity of the chicken with the buckwheat mixture, making sure it is firmly filled. Tie the legs of the chicken together with kitchen string so the buckwheat doesn't escape.

Place the chicken neck-first in a narrow and deep saucepan that fits it snugly. Add the remaining garlic, dates, chestnuts and ginseng, along with the stock, tamari and ginger. You need at least 10 cm of stock to clear the top of the chicken because most of it will be absorbed by the buckwheat.

Bring the soup to a simmer over medium heat, skimming any skum that rises to the top. You don't want to boil the soup too harshly. Cover the pan, reduce the heat and cook for 45 minutes to 1 hour, or until the chicken is cooked. Remove from the heat.

Take the chicken out of the saucepan and pop the bok choy into the hot soup for a few minutes to wilt. Shred the chicken and set aside.

Remove the buckwheat from the chicken cavity and add to the soup, along with the spring onions. Season with salt to taste. Ladle the soup into serving bowls and add the shredded chicken. Garnish with the sesame seeds, Korean chilli paste (if using) and a drizzle of sesame oil.

SERVES 6

TIP

Red dates (jujube), fresh or dried ginseng roots, chestnuts and Korean chilli paste (gochujang) are all available at Asian grocers.

For a nourishing and filling winter meal, I can't go past a Middle Eastern harira soup. This is my favourite version, and while there are a lot of ingredients, it is relatively simple to make. You just need time to let the shanks cook slowly so the meat falls off the bone. I often double this recipe for dinner parties and give the guests a container when they leave. They love it! You will need to start this recipe the day before.

LAMB HARIRA

200 g buckwheat*

2 tablespoons coconut oil

4 lamb shanks

1 large onion, chopped

2 celery stalks, chopped

6 garlic cloves, finely chopped

1 teaspoon ground cumin

1 teaspoon ground turmeric

1 teaspoon ground cinnamon

½ teaspoon ground ginger

¼ teaspoon freshly grated nutmeg

big pinch of saffron threads

400 g can diced tomatoes

2 litres stock or water

2 sweet potatoes (about 300 g in total), diced

sea salt and freshly ground black pepper

270 g pumpkin, diced

2 large courgettes (about 300 g in total), diced

1 bunch of Swiss chard or kale (about 400 g), chopped

1 handful of coriander leaves, chopped

1 handful of flat-leaf parsley leaves, chopped

1 handful of mint leaves, chopped

2 lemons, cut into wedges

See Glossary

Soak the buckwheat overnight in water. The next day, drain well.

Melt the oil in a large saucepan over medium–high heat. Add the lamb shanks and brown on all sides. Remove from the pan and set aside. Reduce the heat to medium and add the onion and celery to the pan. Sauté, stirring occasionally, for about 4–5 minutes, or until the onion is translucent. Add the garlic and spices and sauté for another 1–2 minutes. Stir in the tomatoes and cook for 3–4 minutes. Pour in the stock or water and return the meat to the pan. Bring to the boil, reduce the heat to medium–low and simmer for about 2 hours, or until the meat is falling off the bone. Remove the shanks and allow to cool.

Once the shanks are cool enough to handle, remove the meat and shred roughly. Discard the bones and return the meat to the soup.

Add the buckwheat, sweet potato and salt and pepper to the soup and simmer for 10 minutes. Add the pumpkin and cook for a further 10 minutes before adding the courgette and Swiss chard or kale. Simmer for 10 minutes until all vegetables are cooked. Adjust the seasoning, stir in the coriander, parsley and mint. Serve with lemon wedges for each diner to squeeze into their soup.

SERVES 6

VARIATIONS

Substitute chicken legs, oxtail or beef cheek for the lamb.

Eliminate the meat altogether for a vegetarian version.

Sometimes 2–3 whisked eggs are stirred into the soup at the end, to make it even more delicious.

SALADS +
VEGETABLES

Never underestimate the importance of herbs! And never underestimate how easy it is to grow them in your own backyard or on your balcony. In general, herbs are the leafy parts of any plant used for culinary or medicinal purposes. Spices are usually a dried product from another part of the plant, including seeds, berries, bark, roots and fruits. Herbs have been used since prehistoric times and modern pharmaceuticals have their origins in crude herbal medicines. To this day, some drugs are still extracted as fractionate/isolate compounds from raw herbs and then purified to meet pharmaceutical standards. I think of herbs as Mother Nature's medicine cabinet and, with that in mind, I would like to share with you this delicious herb salad.

HERB SALAD with SUMAC DRESSING

2 large handfuls of coriander leaves

2 large handfuls of flat-leaf parsley leaves

1 large handful of dill leaves

1 handful of tarragon leaves

1 large handful of basil leaves, torn

2 large handfuls of mint leaves

40 g watercress leaves

3 radishes, sliced

100 g almonds, walnuts or pistachio nuts (activated if possible, see page 176), roughly chopped

SUMAC DRESSING

½ teaspoon sea salt

½ teaspoon freshly ground black pepper

1 tablespoon lemon juice

2 tablespoons olive oil

1 teaspoon sumac*

* *See Glossary*

Gently wash all the herb leaves, being careful not to bruise them. Drain in a colander and then dry in a salad spinner or by spreading them over a clean tea towel.

To assemble the salad, place the herbs, watercress and radish in a large bowl.

In a small bowl, mix the dressing ingredients together.

Add the nuts and dressing to the salad and toss gently. Season to taste and serve immediately.

SERVES 4

You can add any veggies
you like, or even some tempeh,
roast chicken, prawns or raw
salmon or tuna, to these
delicious daikon wraps.

The first time I tried daikon (white radish), I was completely blown away by the flavour. Also known as oriental or Chinese radish, its roots and leaves are both edible and nutritious. Just 100 grams of daikon has approximately 35 per cent of your recommended daily vitamin C intake, and it's also an antifungal, an anti-inflammatory and a great digestive aid. You can cook daikon (I like to use it in miso soup) but my favourite way to eat it is raw in a salad. The easiest way to prepare the daikon for these wraps is to slice it with a mandolin (hand slicer) – this way you get the slices paper thin. Add any fresh ingredient you love, or just chop everything up and pop it into a big salad bowl.

DAIKON WRAPS

1 red pepper

1 tablespoon coconut oil, melted

1 large daikon*

1 handful of mixed salad leaves

1 small cucumber, finely sliced

1 large handful of bean sprouts

8 okra*, sliced in half lengthways

1 ripe avocado, halved and sliced lengthways

1 punnet (130 g) enoki mushrooms

2 large handfuls of rocket or spinach leaves

2 tablespoons pine nuts, toasted

toasted black sesame seeds, to serve

GINGER DIPPING SAUCE

200 ml olive oil

150 ml apple cider vinegar* or coconut vinegar*

2 garlic cloves, roughly chopped

2.5 cm piece of ginger, peeled and sliced

1 red Asian shallot, sliced

1 tablespoon tamari*

fish sauce*, to taste

lime juice, to taste

1 tablespoon sesame seeds, toasted

* See Glossary

Preheat the oven to 200°C.

Rub the pepper all over with the oil, place on a baking tray and roast for 15–20 minutes, or until the skin is blistered and the pepper is very soft. Transfer to a bowl and cover with plastic wrap. When cool enough to handle, peel off the skin and remove the seeds and pith. Cut into thin strips.

Thinly slice the daikon lengthways using a mandolin to create about 16 long sheets. Lay them out flat on your work surface. Divide all the salad ingredients and the pine nuts evenly among the sheets of daikon, arranging them along the length so there is some overhang at each end. Roll the daikon around the salad ingredients to form a wrap and cut each one in half. They should stay together quite well, but if not, pop a toothpick into each roll to secure.

To make the dipping sauce, process the oil, vinegar, garlic, ginger, shallot and tamari in a food processor until well combined. Add the fish sauce and lime juice to taste, then stir through the sesame seeds.

Arrange the daikon wraps on a serving plate, overlapped-edges down. The salad leaves and other fillings should peek out over the tops of the wraps and look really pretty. Scatter with black sesame seeds and serve with the dipping sauce on the side.

SERVES 4

This bright salad is bursting with dark leafy greens, which are some of the most nutrient-dense foods around, providing fibre, minerals, vitamins and antioxidants. This recipe calls for a fair bit of chopping, but spending 10 minutes slicing and dicing in the kitchen can be quite meditative after a busy day.

SUPER SUMMER SALAD

2 large handfuls of baby spinach leaves

2 handfuls of rocket

1 large handful of kale, thinly sliced

1 celery stalk, thinly sliced

1 small Lebanese cucumber, roughly chopped

1 large carrot, finely sliced

1 small beetroot, peeled and coarsely grated

3 tablespoons finely chopped flat-leaf parsley leaves

3 tablespoons finely chopped mint leaves

3 tablespoons finely chopped coriander leaves

100 g almonds (activated if possible, see page 176), roughly chopped

AVOCADO DRESSING

1 avocado

3 tablespoons lemon or lime juice

½ garlic clove, crushed

2 tablespoons apple cider vinegar*

sea salt and freshly ground black pepper

3 tablespoons extra-virgin olive oil

* See Glossary

Combine all of the salad ingredients in a serving bowl.

To make the dressing, place the avocado in a bowl and mash well. Add the lemon or lime juice, garlic, apple cider vinegar and salt and pepper to taste. Slowly whisk in the olive oil until it is well combined and creamy.

Just before serving, pour the dressing over the salad and give it a light toss.

SERVES 4

Sweet potatoes, roasted in their skins, are a staple in my home because, as far as starches go, they are one of the most nutritious. I tend to roast about six or more at a time, then I use them up over the next few days in salads, stews, soups and curries – I even take them on planes as a snack!

ROASTED SWEET POTATO WITH GREMOLATA

2 large sweet potatoes, unpeeled

GREMOLATA

finely grated zest of 1 large lemon

1 garlic clove, crushed

⅓ cup chopped flat-leaf parsley leaves

2 teaspoons olive oil

½ teaspoon sea salt

¼ teaspoon freshly ground black pepper

For the gremolata, thoroughly combine all the ingredients in a small bowl, cover with plastic wrap and refrigerate for 1 hour.

Preheat the oven to 100°C.

Place the sweet potatoes on a baking tray and roast for about 6 hours, or until tender. (As all ovens vary, it's a good idea to insert a metal skewer into the potatoes after 4 or 5 hours to check if they are ready.)

Cut the sweet potatoes into pieces and serve tossed with the gremolata.

SERVES 4

VARIATIONS

You could make chimichurri (page 155) or harissa (page 248) to team with the roasted sweet potato. It is also wonderful slathered with duck or chicken liver pâté (page 144) and served with lots of freshly chopped herbs and cultured veggies (see pages 197–209 for more on these).

Watermelon salads are all the rage lately, and I have to admit I love them. Most are served with some form of cheese, but I use cashew cheese with this instead – and it comes out a treat. This recipe was inspired by chef Gavin Baker, my business partner and friend, and it shows how simple ingredients can really shine. Thanks, mate!

WATERMELON AND RADISH SALAD

800 g seedless watermelon

150 ml apple cider vinegar*

40 g pine nuts

1 large handful of pepper leaves*

1 large handful of wild rocket

1 large handful of dandelion leaves*

1 radish, thinly sliced

1 red Asian shallot, finely chopped

1 tablespoon Dijon mustard

1 teaspoon honey

100 ml extra-virgin olive oil

80 ml truffle oil*

50 g Cashew Cheese (page 190)

1 tablespoon balsamic vinegar

pomegranate seeds, to serve

* See Glossary

Cut the watermelon into 3 cm thick slices, then cut these into large pieces and set aside.

Put 80 ml of the apple cider vinegar in a small saucepan and place over medium–high heat. Bring to the boil and reduce for 3–5 minutes, or until about 1 tablespoon of liquid is left. Add the pine nuts, toss to coat and transfer to a tray to cool.

Place the salad leaves in a bowl of iced water for 5–10 minutes to make the leaves nice and crisp. Place the radish in a separate bowl of iced water for 5–10 minutes so that it becomes crisp as well.

To make the dressing, place the remaining apple cider vinegar in a bowl with the shallot, mustard, honey, extra-virgin olive oil and truffle oil and whisk together.

When you are ready to serve, place the watermelon in a bowl. Drain and dry the leaves and radish, then add them to the watermelon. Pour over the dressing and toss to combine. Crumble over the cashew cheese and top with the pine nuts, balsamic vinegar and some pomegranate seeds.

SERVES 4

We usually associate beetroot with salads, juices, burgers, sandwiches, chutneys or relishes, but it also makes a wonderful base for a curry. Beetroot is a good vegetable source of iron, which is great for boosting energy. It also has large amounts of folic acid, which is beneficial for brain function. The best way to eat beetroot is raw, to maximise nutrient value and absorption, but cooked in a delicious curry, like this Sri Lankan–inspired one, it is rewarding on so many levels.

SRI LANKAN BEETROOT AND EGG CURRY

1 kg beetroot, trimmed, peeled and cut into 2 cm cubes

1 teaspoon chilli powder

2 teaspoons ground coriander

1 teaspoon sea salt

2 tablespoons finely chopped coriander roots and stems

2 cinnamon sticks, broken up

2 long green chillies, finely sliced

1 × 10 cm piece of pandan leaf* (optional)

20 curry leaves*

2 tablespoons coconut oil

1 large red onion, finely chopped

4 garlic cloves, finely chopped

1½ tablespoons apple cider vinegar* or coconut vinegar*

700 ml coconut milk

honey, to taste (optional)

8 soft-boiled eggs, peeled and halved (for instructions on soft-boiling eggs, see page 26)

150 ml coconut cream, plus extra, to serve (optional)

coriander leaves, to serve

fried shallots (for a recipe, see page 252), to serve

* See Glossary

Mix the beetroot, chilli powder, ground coriander, salt, chopped coriander, cinnamon sticks, green chilli, pandan leaf (if using) and curry leaves in a bowl and set aside.

Melt the coconut oil in a saucepan over medium heat. Add the onion and garlic and fry until translucent, stirring occasionally. Add the beetroot mixture and vinegar and stir to combine. Pour in the coconut milk and simmer for 30–40 minutes, or until the sauce has reduced a little. To test if the curry is completely cooked, stick a knife through a piece of beetroot. It should fall apart quite easily but still have a slight crunch to it. If the sauce becomes too thick, add a little water.

Check the taste of the curry. If there is too much vinegar, add a bit of honey to balance it. Add the eggs, reserving 4 halves to garnish. Add the coconut cream and stir to combine. Cook for 2 minutes, or until the sauce is thick and glossy. Remove from the heat.

Spoon the curry into bowls and top with the remaining eggs. Drizzle over the extra coconut cream (if using) and top with coriander leaves and fried shallots.

SERVES 4 HUNGRY PEOPLE

Asian cucumber salads are one of the most refreshing dishes, especially when you team them with a hearty curry or spicy stir-fry. Cucumber is 95 per cent water yet is full of potassium, magnesium and fibre. I often add cultured vegetables to cucumber salads as they complement each other nicely.

CUCUMBER SALAD WITH AVOCADO AND GINGER

100 g red or black quinoa*, rinsed

1 small red onion, very finely sliced

2 cm piece of ginger, peeled and sliced

1 teaspoon sea salt

2 large garlic cloves, peeled

4 small cucumbers (about 600 g in total), peeled

1 tablespoon sesame seeds, toasted

3 tablespoons chopped coriander leaves

1 tomato, diced

1 avocado, sliced

SESAME DRESSING

3 tablespoons apple cider vinegar*

2 teaspoons honey (optional)

2 tablespoons olive oil

2 teaspoons sesame oil

* See Glossary

Place the quinoa in a small saucepan with 350 ml of water and bring to the boil. Reduce the heat and simmer for 15 minutes, or until the water has been absorbed. Set aside to cool.

To make the dressing, whisk all the ingredients in a bowl. Add the onion, mix well and set aside to marinate for about an hour.

Place the ginger and salt in a mortar and pound well with a pestle. Add the garlic and continue pounding until well crushed and broken into pieces (stop pounding before it disintegrates into a puree). Use a spatula to scrape the contents of the mortar into the bowl with the onion and dressing. Stir together.

Cut the cucumbers in half lengthways, then cut each half on an angle into 5 mm thick slices. Add the cucumber to the bowl, followed by the sesame seeds and coriander leaves. Stir well and leave to sit for 10 minutes.

Before serving, stir the salad again, drain some of the liquid that has accumulated at the bottom of the bowl and adjust the seasoning. Toss in the tomato, quinoa and avocado and serve.

SERVES 4–6

Try mixing some cultured veggies through this salad (see pages 197–209).

Carrots really are a wonder food. Eaten raw or cooked, they contain lots of essential vitamins as well as potassium and fibre. One carrot alone contains twice the recommended daily intake of vitamin A, which is essential for maintaining healthy eyes. Carrots also contain vitamins K and C: vitamin K contributes to bone strength as well as kidney health; vitamin C is useful, as we know, for the immune system, but also helps your body to absorb iron.

CARROTS WITH KALE AND HARISSA

500 g baby carrots, halved lengthways

2 tablespoons coconut oil, melted

pinch of ground cumin

sea salt and freshly ground black pepper

1 bunch of kale (about 450 g), central stalks removed

3 garlic cloves, finely chopped

1 tablespoon harissa (for a recipe, see page 248)

60 g almonds (activated if possible, see page 176), chopped

grated zest of ½ lemon (optional)

Preheat the oven to 180°C.

Toss the carrot in 1 tablespoon of the coconut oil and cumin, season with salt and pepper and roast for about 15 minutes, or until tender.

Pour about 1 cm of water into a saucepan and bring to the boil. Add the kale and stir constantly for about 1 minute, or until the kale softens. Drain and run cold water over the kale until cool. Dry the kale and finely chop.

Heat the remaining coconut oil and garlic in a large frying pan over medium–high heat for about 2 minutes. Make sure you stir continuously, as you don't want the garlic to brown. Remove from the heat and stir in the harissa, carrot and kale. Add the almonds, a scant ½ teaspoon of salt and the lemon zest (if using) and stir again gently until everything is well combined. Serve warm or at room temperature.

SERVES 4

TIP

Carrots come in many varieties; orange has always been popular, but you can also get yellow, purple and red. I always try to seek out organically grown and heirloom varieties whenever possible.

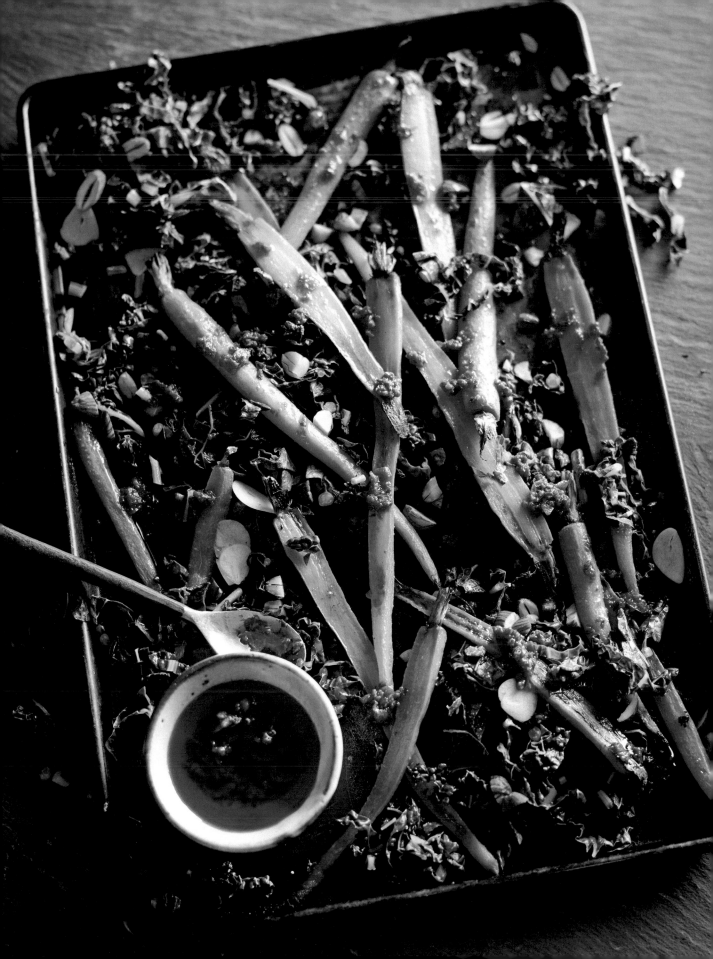

In summer, there is nothing better than a simple bowl of courgette noodles, seasoned and tossed with some olive oil and served with lashings of gorgeous, full-flavoured tomato sauce. This recipe will leave you feeling so clean and refreshed – not bloated like many people feel after eating a bowl of pasta.

COURGETTE NOODLES WITH RICH TOMATO SAUCE

6–10 semi-dried tomatoes

2 tomatoes, roughly chopped

1 red pepper, roughly chopped

6–10 green olives, pitted and roughly chopped

125 g Swiss brown mushrooms, roughly chopped

1 large handful of basil leaves, torn

1 teaspoon finely chopped rosemary leaves

2 garlic cloves, finely chopped

1 small red chilli, sliced (optional)

squeeze of lemon juice

80 ml olive oil

4 courgettes

1 tablespoon finely chopped flat-leaf parsley leaves

freshly ground black pepper

1 large handful of baby spinach leaves

toasted pine nuts, to serve

sunflower seeds, to serve

pumpkin seeds, to serve

Place the semi-dried tomatoes in a food processor, along with the fresh tomatoes, pepper, olives, mushrooms, basil, rosemary, garlic, chilli (if using) and lemon juice. Pulse until combined but still chunky. Transfer to a bowl, drizzle on 3 tablespoons of olive oil, then set aside for 5–10 minutes to marinate.

To make the courgette noodles, thinly slice the courgette using a mandolin or a vegetable peeler. Toss the courgette with the remaining oil, the parsley and some pepper and set aside to marinate for 5 minutes at room temperature.

To serve, combine the courgette noodles with the chunky tomato sauce and baby spinach leaves, then scatter with pine nuts, sunflower seeds and pumpkin seeds.

SERVES 4

Root vegetables have a calming and restorative effect on the digestive system, which is why I love to include them, either cooked or raw, in as many recipes as I can. This recipe can be used as a guide – play around with the ingredients until you find what suits you in terms of time, budget and taste. It has some similar ingredients to a classic coleslaw, but is not slathered in mayonnaise. You can serve this with yoghurt or sour cream, but I like to keep it simple with a dressing of apple cider vinegar, lemon juice, olive oil and lots of herbs. This slaw is good enough to eat on its own and is great served with grilled fish or fried chicken. It is also wonderful on scrambled eggs for breakfast.

ROOT VEGETABLE SLAW

3 beetroot

2 carrots

½ celeriac

1 kohlrabi

¼ red cabbage, shredded

1 large handful of sliced fennel

2 large handfuls of coriander leaves, roughly chopped

2 large handfuls of mint leaves, shredded

2 handfuls of flat-leaf parsley leaves, roughly chopped

½ tablespoon finely grated lemon zest

1 teaspoon freshly ground black pepper

DRESSING

80 ml lemon juice

80 ml olive oil

3 tablespoons apple cider vinegar*

2 teaspoons honey (optional)

1 teaspoon sea salt

* *See Glossary*

Peel the beetroot, carrots, celeriac and kohlrabi and slice thinly, about 2 mm thick. Stack a few slices at a time on top of each other and cut them into matchstick-like strips. Alternatively, use a mandolin or a food processor with the appropriate attachment. Place all the strips in a large bowl with the cabbage and fennel and cover with cold water. Set aside while you make the dressing.

To make the dressing, place all the ingredients in a small saucepan over low–medium heat. Bring to a gentle simmer and stir until the salt has dissolved. Remove from the heat.

Drain the vegetables and dry well with paper towel. Dry the bowl and replace the vegetable strips. Pour the hot dressing over the vegetables and mix well. Place in the fridge for at least 45 minutes.

When ready to serve, add the herbs, lemon zest and pepper to the salad. Toss well, taste and add more salt if needed. Pile onto serving plates and serve.

SERVES 4

About a decade ago, molecular gastronomy took the culinary world by storm. We saw chefs changing the composition of food and playing with our senses the way a magician challenges our beliefs about what is possible. One dish that gained notoriety was cauliflower rice – great for anyone wishing to avoid grains and wheat. So here is a play on the ever-popular fried rice. I've replaced bland white rice with nutrient-rich, flavoursome and healthy cauliflower, and added all your favourite ingredients: tamari, egg, veggies, prawns, herbs, ginger and garlic. Isn't it great that, unlike magicians, chefs are happy to share their secrets?

CAULIFLOWER FRIED RICE

1½ cauliflower heads (about 1 kg), separated into florets

4 slices of bacon or ham, diced

4 eggs, whisked

2 tablespoons coconut oil

1 onion, finely chopped

2 garlic cloves, finely chopped

200 g shelled and deveined small raw prawns

100 g shiitake or oyster mushrooms, sliced

2.5 cm piece of ginger, finely grated

100 g okra*, sliced

100 g brussels sprouts, finely sliced

2 tablespoons tamari*

1 large handful of bean sprouts

2 spring onions, finely sliced

1 long red chilli, finely sliced

2 tablespoons chopped coriander leaves

2 tablespoons chopped flat-leaf parsley leaves

1 tablespoon chopped mint leaves

sea salt and freshly ground white pepper

kimchi (for a recipe, see page 208), to serve

fish sauce*, to serve

* See Glossary

Pulse the cauliflower in a food processor until it resembles rice.

In a large frying pan or wok, fry the bacon over high heat until crispy. Remove and set aside.

Tip the eggs into the pan and tilt the pan so that the egg covers the base. Cook for a couple of minutes, or until the egg is set. Remove, slice into thin strips and set aside.

Heat the coconut oil in the pan over high heat, add the onion and garlic and cook for a few minutes, or until softened. Stir in the prawns, mushrooms and ginger and cook for another few minutes. Add the okra and brussels sprouts and cook for 1 minute. Add the cauliflower and cook for 2–3 minutes, or until tender. Add the bacon, egg, tamari, sprouts, spring onion, chilli, herbs and some salt and pepper and cook for 2 minutes, or until everything is heated through and well combined.

Serve with some kimchi and a splash of fish sauce.

SERVES 6

Kale definitely deserves the title 'nutritional powerhouse' – it's rich in iron, calcium, antioxidants and fibre.

Kale is jam-packed with nutrients and is so versatile. It works well in salads, juices and smoothies, and is delicious when made into kale chips (page 180). This is a gorgeous salad that can be whipped up in a matter of minutes. Serve it as a side or add some chicken, lamb, prawns or other seafood and enjoy it for lunch or dinner.

KALE SALAD WITH FENNEL AND SUNFLOWER SEEDS

2 bunches of kale (about 800 g), central stalks removed and thinly sliced

2½ tablespoons olive oil

1 large fennel bulb, thinly sliced

4 radishes, thinly sliced

100 g sunflower seeds, toasted

SEEDED MUSTARD DRESSING

80 ml Fermented Mustard (page 203)

80 ml lemon juice

100 ml olive oil

sea salt and freshly ground black pepper

To make the dressing, place the mustard and lemon juice in a bowl and whisk together. Slowly whisk in the olive oil until well combined. Season with salt and pepper.

Place the kale in a large bowl and pour over the olive oil. Rub the oil into the kale with your hands – almost like you are massaging the kale. This removes the waxy coating from the kale and allows it to absorb the dressing. Pour the dressing over the kale, toss and leave to stand for at least 30 minutes before serving.

Just before serving, toss in the fennel, radishes and sunflower seeds and adjust the seasoning if necessary.

SERVES 4–6

Leek is an under-utilised vegetable that adds a lovely sweetness to dishes when sautéed as the base of a soup or braise. It is also one of my favourite ingredients to add to salads as I find it a lot more palatable when cooked than, say, raw onion. The combination here of beetroot, leek and walnuts with fresh herbs and a spicy dressing is something to really savour and enjoy. This salad works beautifully on its own or marries perfectly with seafood or grilled steak. You could even add some soft-boiled eggs and have it for brekkie!

SPICY BEETROOT, LEEK AND WALNUT SALAD

4 beetroot

1 teaspoon ground cumin

1 tablespoon coconut oil, melted

sea salt and freshly ground black pepper

4 small leeks, white part only, cut into 10 cm segments

1 handful of coriander leaves, roughly chopped

1 small handful of mint leaves

1 small handful of flat-leaf parsley leaves

1 small handful of dill

2 large handfuls of rocket

2 tablespoons sunflower seeds, toasted

1 handful of pomegranate seeds (about 50 g) (optional)

DRESSING

100 g walnuts, roughly chopped

1 garlic clove, finely chopped

¼ teaspoon dried chilli flakes

3 tablespoons apple cider vinegar*

½ teaspoon walnut oil

2 ½ tablespoons extra-virgin olive oil

1 teaspoon sea salt

* See Glossary

Preheat the oven to 220°C.

Place each beetroot on a piece of foil. Sprinkle with the cumin, drizzle over the coconut oil and add some salt and pepper. Wrap up and roast in the oven for about 1 hour, depending on their size. They are cooked when you are able to stick a small knife through to the centre easily. Remove from the oven and set aside.

When cool enough to handle, peel and halve each beetroot then cut into 1 cm thick wedges. Put in a bowl and set aside.

Place the leek in a saucepan of salted water, bring to the boil, reduce the heat and simmer for 10 minutes, or until just cooked. (Don't overcook them or they will fall apart.) Drain and refresh under cold water, then use a very sharp, serrated knife to cut each segment into three smaller pieces. Pat dry, transfer to a separate bowl and set aside.

While the beetroot and leek are cooking, mix all the dressing ingredients together.

Combine the herbs in a serving bowl and toss gently, then add the beetroot and leek.

Toss the salad with the dressing or serve the dressing on the side. Garnish with the sunflower seeds and pomegranate seeds (if using).

SERVES 4

Roasted seasonal vegetables are a staple in my house. I try to do a couple of baking trays so there are heaps left over for breakfast, lunch and dinner the next day. Once you have a great base of vegetables, there are endless ways to jazz them up. Use them in a delicious salad with a simple dressing of apple cider vinegar and macadamia nut oil, or try this beautiful dressing below; pop them into a gorgeous stock to make a soup; add them to a curry or braise; or simply serve them as a side dish.

ROASTED VEGETABLES WITH TAHINI AND ZA'ATAR

1 large butternut pumpkin, unpeeled and cut into 2 cm wedges

2 sweet potatoes, diced

3 parsnips, cut into quarters lengthways

8–10 brussels sprouts, blanched

2 red onions, cut into 3 cm thick wedges

3 tablespoons coconut oil, melted

sea salt and freshly ground black pepper

2 handfuls of rocket (optional)

2 tablespoons toasted pine nuts

1 tablespoon za'atar*

1 tablespoon roughly chopped flat-leaf parsley leaves

1 handful of green Sicilian olives or kalamata olives

DRESSING

3 tablespoons hulled tahini*

1½ tablespoons lemon juice

1 small garlic clove, crushed

¼ teaspoon sea salt

* See Glossary

Preheat the oven to 200°C.

Place the pumpkin, sweet potato, parsnip, brussels sprouts and onion in a large bowl. Add the coconut oil, 1 teaspoon of salt and a little pepper and toss well. Spread on a baking tray and roast for 30–40 minutes, or until the vegetables have taken on some colour and are cooked through. Keep an eye on the onion as it might cook faster than the pumpkin and need to be removed earlier. Remove from the oven and leave to cool.

To make the dressing, place the tahini in a small bowl along with the lemon juice, 2 tablespoons of water, the garlic and salt. Whisk until the dressing is the consistency of honey, adding more water or tahini if necessary.

To serve, spread the vegetables out on a large serving platter. Top with the rocket (if using) and drizzle over the dressing. Sprinkle the pine nuts on top, followed by the za'atar, parsley and olives.

SERVES 4

TIP

Play around with different seasonal vegetables from your local farmers market. Some of my favourites are beetroot, parsnip, sweet potato, pumpkin, carrot, courgette, brussels sprouts, garlic, chilli, aubergine, pepper, corn, asparagus, mushrooms, okra, cauliflower, broccoli, olives, swede, turnip and kale.

SEAFOOD

This is a showstopper of a dish, but is not at all difficult to make. I always have small portions of prawns, scallops, salmon, kingfish and tuna belly in the freezer, and pull out a packet in the morning and pop it in the fridge to thaw throughout the day. When I get home, I simply slice the seafood (the scallops slice more easily if they are still frozen), cut the veg, quickly make the dressing and toss it all together. Please play around with this – it also works extremely well with sliced ripe tomatoes for a vegan alternative.

KINGFISH SASHIMI WITH YUZU DRESSING

400 g kingfish or other sashimi-grade fish fillet (I also like oysters, salmon, tuna and prawns)

1 green jalapeno chilli, finely sliced

1 avocado, finely diced

1 Lebanese cucumber, finely diced

1 radish, finely sliced into rounds

1 tablespoon salmon roe

1 teaspoon black and white sesame seeds, toasted

baby shiso leaves* (optional)

YUZU DRESSING

3 tablespoons yuzu juice*

3 tablespoons tamari*

3 tablespoons extra-virgin olive oil

2 teaspoons sesame oil

1 tablespoon finely julienned ginger

pinch of freshly ground white pepper

* See Glossary

To make the dressing, combine the yuzu juice, tamari, olive oil, sesame oil, ginger and white pepper in a jar and shake well. Thinly slice the fish and arrange on a plate. Scatter on the chilli, avocado, cucumber and radish. Pour the dressing over the fish and finish with the salmon roe, sesame seeds and shiso leaves (if using).

SERVES 4

TIP

If you can't find yuzu juice, you can substitute with the same quantity of fresh lemon, lime, grapefruit or orange juice, or the juice of any other citrus fruit.

Could you imagine having grilled or fried fish and chips without lemon? Or how about oysters without a vinaigrette made with tart vinegar or fresh lemon? One of my favourite ways to serve seafood is to let it sit for a day or two in a pickle mix to develop some wonderful flavours. You can experiment with mussels, sardines, tuna, salmon, white fish and oysters, and play around with different spices and flavour profiles. This is a simple yet elegant entree to serve to guests, as the prawns look great in glass jars.

QUICK PICKLED PRAWNS

700 g raw king prawns

1 small fennel bulb, finely sliced, fennel fronds reserved

¼ red onion, finely sliced

2 garlic cloves, finely sliced

½ long red chilli, finely sliced

4 small radishes, finely sliced

125 ml lemon juice

3 tablespoons apple cider vinegar*

80 ml extra-virgin olive oil

pinch of sumac*

sea salt and freshly ground black pepper

aïoli (for a recipe, see page 252) or mayonnaise, to serve

* See Glossary

Cook the prawns in a saucepan of boiling salted water for a couple of minutes, or until just cooked. Plunge into iced water to stop the cooking process. Peel and devein the prawns, leaving the tails intact.

Mix all the remaining ingredients together in a bowl. Add the prawns and place in the fridge for up to 2 days or serve immediately with homemade aïoli or good mayonnaise.

SERVES 2

If you don't feel like rolling these yourself, simply pop all the ingredients in small bowls on the table and let your family roll their own!

Who doesn't love Japanese food? I know everyone in my family does and that's why this recipe features every week in our home – sometimes twice a week when the weather is warmer. My tip is to place all your ingredients in bowls on the table and let everyone roll their own. This is how we do it, and we have discovered that the kids try things they normally wouldn't. Just by having new ingredients in front of them and explaining what they are, they might try a wrap with a little bit of kimchi or some fennel.

INDII'S NORI ROLLS

400 g sashimi-grade fish such as salmon or tuna, sliced into 1 cm strips

1 avocado, sliced

2 large handfuls of rocket

½ cucumber, julienned

½ carrot, julienned

¼ fennel bulb, shaved

¼ small daikon*, julienned

2 tablespoons black and white sesame seeds, toasted

50 g salmon roe

1 tablespoon dulse flakes* (optional)

100 g kimchi (for a recipe, see page 208) (optional)

4 toasted nori sheets*

tamari*, to serve

SPICY MAYONNAISE

4 tablespoons mayonnaise

1 tablespoon Fermented Hot Chilli Sauce (page 209) or wasabi*

1 teaspoon finely grated ginger

1 teaspoon sesame seeds, toasted

¼ teaspoon sesame oil

* See Glossary

To make the spicy mayonnaise, mix all the ingredients in a bowl.

Place the fish, avocado, vegetables, sesame seeds, salmon roe, dulse flakes and kimchi (if using) into separate bowls, ready to assemble. Cut the nori sheets in half to create 10 cm × 18 cm sheets.

Place a nori sheet in the palm of your hand, shiny side down, and add a slice of fish, 1 teaspoon of the spicy mayonnaise and whatever other fillings take your fancy. Fold a bottom corner of the nori over the filling and then roll up to form a cone shape. Serve immediately with the tamari as a dipping sauce.

SERVES 4 AS A STARTER

VARIATIONS

Try some sliced pepper or raw beans, or perhaps some blanched broccolini or raw sliced kale. Canned tuna is a great substitute, or some quinoa-crumbed fish (page 111).

This classic Middle Eastern dish is one I love serving at dinner parties. It is always a crowd-pleaser and is so easy to make. Tahini, a paste made from sesame seeds, is jam-packed with good stuff, including vitamin E, potassium, magnesium and small amounts of calcium and fibre. I wouldn't eat tahini on a daily basis, but as a treat from time to time, the flavour it adds to dressings and sauces is great. If you can tolerate dairy, you can also add some yoghurt to the tahini dressing, which will make it creamier and lighter.

SALMON WITH POMEGRANATE AND HERBS

1 × 1.2 kg side fillet of salmon, skin left on and pin-boned

2 tablespoons coconut oil

sea salt and freshly ground black pepper

seeds of 1 pomegranate, to serve

pomegranate molasses*, to serve (optional)

TAHINI DRESSING

350 g unhulled tahini*

100 ml lemon juice

2 teaspoons ground cumin

2 garlic cloves, crushed

HERB CRUST

1 red onion, finely chopped

2 very large handfuls of coriander leaves, finely chopped

2 large handfuls of flat-leaf parsley leaves, finely chopped

1 large handful of mint leaves, finely chopped

3 long red chillies, finely chopped

100 g almonds (activated if possible, see page 176), finely chopped

100 g walnuts (activated if possible, see page 176), finely chopped

2 tablespoons sumac*

150 ml olive oil

* See Glossary

Preheat the oven to 70°C.

Rub the salmon all over with the coconut oil and season with salt and pepper. Wrap the salmon in baking paper, leaving the seam on top and twisting the ends to seal. Tie kitchen string around the paper in three different places. Place the wrapped salmon on a baking tray and bake for 30–45 minutes, or until it is slightly pink in the centre.

Meanwhile, to make the tahini dressing, place all the ingredients in a food processor with 80 ml of water. Process to form a thick sauce.

To make the herb crust, combine all the ingredients in a bowl and season with salt and pepper.

Remove the salmon from the paper and transfer to a serving platter. Spread some tahini dressing on top, then cover with the herb crust. Sprinkle on the pomegranate seeds and drizzle over a little pomegranate molasses (if using). Serve with the remaining tahini dressing on the side.

SERVES 6

I cannot go past asparagus when it is in season. It is so versatile to use in the home kitchen: whether you steam it with some seafood, turn it into soup, stir-fry it for your favourite Asian dish, sauté it to serve with eggs for breakfast or grill it on the barbie to serve as part of a vegetable platter. This recipe was inspired by the wonderful chef Ravi Kapur in San Francisco, with whom I've had the pleasure of working. He's elevated a simple caesar dressing into something memorable by adding bonito flakes, giving it a lovely umami flavour. You can use any grilled seafood or even chicken in this dish instead of tuna.

TUNA AND ASPARAGUS WITH BONITO CAESAR DRESSING

4 small yellow or red beetroot

2 tablespoons coconut oil

sea salt and freshly ground black pepper

12 asparagus spears

600 g tuna, sliced into four pieces

2 tablespoons black and white sesame seeds, toasted

1 tablespoon sunflower seeds, toasted

bonito flakes*, to serve

1 handful of baby shiso leaves*, to serve

BONITO CAESAR DRESSING

1 egg

1 egg yolk

1 tablespoon Dijon mustard

2 tablespoons yuzu juice*

3 anchovies, finely chopped

3 big pinches of bonito flakes*

450 ml olive oil

sea salt and freshly ground white pepper

* See Glossary

Preheat the oven to 170°C.

Rub the beetroot with ½ tablespoon of the coconut oil and sprinkle with salt and pepper. Wrap the beetroot in foil and roast for 20 minutes, or until tender. Leave to cool, peel, then slice thinly and set aside.

To make the bonito caesar dressing, place the egg, egg yolk, mustard, yuzu juice, anchovies and bonito flakes in a food processor and pulse to blend. With the motor running, add the oil in a thin, steady stream. After a minute or two, the mixture will emulsify into a thick sauce. Stop adding the oil when it has reached your desired consistency (you may not need to use all the oil). If the dressing is too thick, you can thin it with a little bit of water. Adjust the flavour by adding more yuzu juice or mustard, if desired, and season with salt and pepper. Set aside.

Heat a barbecue or frying pan to high. Coat the asparagus in ½ tablespoon of the coconut oil and cook for 2–4 minutes, or until just tender. Set aside.

Season the tuna. Add the remaining tablespoon of coconut oil to the barbecue or frying pan and cook the tuna for 30–60 seconds on each side.

To serve, dollop 2 tablespoons of dressing onto each plate. Cut the tuna into 5 mm thick slices and place on top. Arrange the beetroot and asparagus next to the tuna. Sprinkle over the sesame and sunflower seeds, bonito flakes and shiso leaves.

SERVES 4

TIP

Yellow varieties of beetroot are often available at farmers markets, but if you can't find any, red beetroot are absolutely fine.

Every once in a while a recipe comes along that stops me in my tracks. This happened recently up on the Sunshine Coast in Queensland when we went to well-respected chef David Rayner's Noosaville restaurant, Thomas Corner. For entree I couldn't go past his barbecued sardines with spiced almonds and saffron mayonnaise. I think if everyone could try these sardines, then everyone would be hooked (pardon the pun), so I asked David and his head chef, Seb, for the recipe. Thanks, guys, we look forward to dining at yours again soon. This recipe needs to be started the day before.

THOMAS CORNER SARDINES

2 garlic cloves, finely chopped

½ long red chilli, finely chopped

80 ml olive oil

10 whole sardines, cleaned

coconut oil, for cooking

watercress, to serve

lemon segments, to serve (see tips)

flat-leaf parsley leaves, to serve

oregano leaves, to serve

½ preserved lemon, skin cut into thin strips, to serve (optional)

extra-virgin olive oil, to serve

sea salt and freshly ground black pepper

PAPRIKA ALMONDS

40 g blanched almonds, toasted

½ teaspoon sea salt

1 teaspoon smoked paprika

1 teaspoon coconut oil

SAFFRON MAYONNAISE

small pinch of saffron threads

1 teaspoon lemon juice

100 g mayonnaise

PICKLED ONION

125 ml red wine vinegar

2 thyme sprigs

6 black peppercorns

1 red onion, sliced into rings

Mix the garlic, chilli and oil in a bowl and spoon into the belly cavities of the fish. Transfer to a container, cover and place in the fridge overnight to marinate.

To make the paprika almonds, toss all the ingredients in a frying pan over medium heat and cook until the nuts are coated and fragrant.

To make the saffron mayonnaise, place the saffron threads and lemon juice in a small bowl for 10 minutes, to soften the saffron. Once soft, combine the mayonnaise, saffron and lemon juice in a bowl and mix well.

To make the pickled onion, combine the vinegar, thyme and peppercorns in a saucepan and bring to the boil. Let the mix cool, then add the onion and marinate for 5–10 minutes.

Heat a chargrill pan or barbecue to high and add a little coconut oil. Grill the sardines for 2 minutes on each side, or until just cooked. Season with salt and pepper.

To serve, place the watercress on a plate and top with the sardines, lemon segments, paprika almonds, pickled onion, some dots of saffron mayonnaise, parsley and oregano leaves and preserved lemon (if using). Drizzle with extra-virgin olive oil and season with salt and pepper.

SERVES 2–4

TIPS

If sardines aren't your cup of tea, try this recipe with fillets of any fish you love, or even prawns or scallops.

To segment a lemon, first remove the zest and white pith. Use a small, sharp knife to cut alongside the membrane of one segment to the centre of the lemon. Cut along the other side of the segment and you should be able to remove the segment. Repeat this process for the remaining segments.

Okra, okra, okra! I think that has a better ring to it than Aussie, Aussie, Aussie! Just kidding. But let me tell you some things about this often overlooked vegetable. Originating from the Middle East, okra is a mucilaginous (meaning slimy) vegetable, which makes it extremely good for the digestive system. Apparently, okra has anti-diabetic properties (its viscous carbs slow the uptake of glucose) and, like any food high in soluble fibre, it can help to lower cholesterol. Okra is also an excellent detoxifier and is high in vitamin C, vitamin B6 and folic acid. Oh, and the most important thing? It tastes bloody good. Now let me hear you: Okra, Okra, Okra; Oi, Oi, Oi!

SEAFOOD WITH ROASTED OKRA, TOMATO AND OLIVES

4 tablespoons coconut oil

1½ teaspoons coriander seeds

1 onion, finely sliced

2 red peppers, cut into 1 cm wide strips

1 long red chilli, halved, seeded and chopped

2 large handfuls of flat-leaf parsley leaves, chopped

2 large handfuls of coriander leaves, chopped

600 g chopped fresh or canned tomatoes

1 teaspoon sweet paprika

sea salt

300 g mussels, scrubbed and debearded

200 g squid, sliced

400 g raw prawns, shelled and deveined

300 g okra* (fresh or frozen)

2 tablespoons finely chopped preserved lemon skin

15 black olives, pitted and halved

1½ tablespoons lemon juice

mint leaves, to serve

* See Glossary

Preheat the oven to 200°C.

Heat 2 tablespoons of the coconut oil in a large saucepan over medium heat. Add the coriander seeds and onion and sauté, stirring occasionally, for 10 minutes, or until the onion softens without colouring. Add the peppers, chilli, parsley and half the chopped coriander. Cook and stir for a further 5 minutes. Next, add the tomatoes, 200 ml of water, the paprika and salt. Reduce the heat to low, cover and simmer for 15 minutes. Add the mussels, squid and prawns and cook, uncovered, for about 5 minutes, or until the sauce is thick and has lost most of the excess liquid.

While the tomato sauce is cooking, prepare the okra. If you are using frozen okra, the stalks will already be removed. If you are using fresh okra, take a small pointy knife and, trying not to cut too low, carefully remove the stalk end, making sure the seeds are not exposed. Discard the stalks and mix the okra with the remaining oil and some salt and spread out in a roasting tin. Roast for 15–20 minutes, or until just tender but still firm.

Add the roasted okra to the tomato sauce. Stir gently and mix in the preserved lemon, olives and half of the remaining chopped coriander. Taste and adjust the seasoning.

Mix in the lemon juice just before serving and garnish with the remaining coriander and mint leaves.

SERVES 4

I love grilling prawns as I find the gentle cooking process helps them to retain their flavour and moisture. You can play around with different dressings to go with the prawns, and you can always rely on the classic cocktail sauce as a favourite to fall back on.

GRILLED PRAWNS WITH CHILLI AND OREGANO

16 raw king prawns, heads removed and deveined

150 ml coconut oil, melted

2 tablespoons dried oregano

2 tablespoons chopped oregano leaves

1 tablespoon dried chilli flakes

2 tablespoons chopped flat-leaf parsley leaves

finely grated zest of 1 lemon

1 garlic clove, finely chopped

sea salt and freshly ground black pepper

lime halves, to serve

Cut the prawns lengthways, almost right through the flesh and along their entire length, leaving the shells and tails on.

Mix the coconut oil with the dried and fresh oregano, the chilli, parsley, lemon zest, garlic and some salt and pepper. Brush over the prawns.

Heat a barbecue or chargrill pan to high. Cook the prawns, shell-side down, for 3 minutes, then turn over and quickly cook for about 10 seconds. Serve with lime halves.

SERVES 4

TIP

This marinade is also great with any type of fish, chicken, steak or anything else that you like to throw on the barbie!

Ceviche, a dish from Central and South America, is one of my favourite raw dishes. The premise for a raw diet is that the most healthy food for the body is uncooked. Although most food is eaten raw, heating food is acceptable as long as the temperature stays below 40–45°C. Cooking is thought to denature the enzymes naturally present in food. According to raw foodists, enzymes are the life force of food, aiding digestion and the absorption of nutrients. At every meal I make sure that at least half of what I'm eating is entirely raw and whenever I am feeling lethargic, I will do a whole day of raw food to re-energise myself.

NIC'S CEVICHE WITH THE WORKS

200 g quinoa*, rinsed

600 g finest-quality fish fillet, such as snapper, tuna or mackerel

1 teaspoon sea salt

juice of 4 limes

4 tablespoons olive oil

2 tablespoons apple cider vinegar*

1 small red onion, finely chopped

1 celery stalk, sliced

1 fennel bulb, shaved

1 red pepper, diced

5 cm piece of ginger, finely grated

2 garlic cloves, finely chopped

1–2 long green or red chillies, finely chopped (seeded or not, as you prefer)

4 tomatoes, cored and finely diced

½ Lebanese cucumber, sliced

1 large avocado, diced

2–3 handfuls of coriander leaves

2 handfuls of rocket

2 purple or yellow witlof, leaves separated and torn

3 tablespoons chopped almonds (activated if possible, see page 176)

1 tablespoon sesame seeds, toasted

See Glossary

Place the quinoa in a saucepan and add 650 ml water. Bring to the boil over high heat, then reduce the heat, cover and cook for 15–20 minutes, or until all the water is absorbed. Place the quinoa in a bowl or spread it on a tray and allow to cool.

Cut the fish into 2 cm cubes and place in a large, shallow dish. Sprinkle with the salt and pour over the lime juice. Leave to marinate for 10 minutes, turning once.

Whisk the olive oil and apple cider vinegar together in a small bowl to make a simple dressing.

In a large serving bowl, mix the quinoa with all of the remaining ingredients. Pour over the dressing and add the fish. Check and adjust the seasoning, then serve.

SERVES 4

TIP

Play with different ingredients in your preparation – just remember to marinate the seafood in a good acidic dressing of lime, lemon or grapefruit juice or a quality vinegar, and off you go!

You can whip up this ceviche in 30 minutes, and it's the perfect meal for a hot summer's day!

I recently travelled to Malaysia and, wanting to immerse myself in the local culture, thought the classic fish head soup would be the best way to jump in – head first! The complexity of flavours that comes from this preparation is amazing, and it is so cheap. I make this after I have visited the fish markets. I usually get a few whole fish filleted for me on the spot (whole fish are generally fresher than the fillets on offer – and if you order the whole fish, you get to keep the head and frame for stocks and soups). As far as health benefits go, the head is high in iodine and fat-soluble vitamins.

MALAYSIAN FISH HEAD CURRY

1 tablespoon tamarind pulp*

3 tablespoons coconut oil

12 Vietnamese mint leaves

20 okra*, diagonally cut into halves

600 g fish heads, such as barramundi or snapper

300 g Asian greens, such as Chinese broccoli (gai larn) or bok choy, chopped

sea salt

1 tablespoon finely grated ginger

1 handful of coriander leaves

1 handful of Vietnamese mint leaves

Cauliflower Rice (page 248), to serve

LEMONGRASS PASTE

1–2 lemongrass stems, white part only, cut into small pieces

1 × 5 cm piece of fresh turmeric, peeled and sliced

½ tablespoon black peppercorns

CHILLI PASTE

6–8 dried red chillies, seeded

2 red Asian shallots, chopped

1 teaspoon shrimp paste (belacan)*

* See Glossary

First, prepare the lemongrass paste. Use a mortar and pestle to pound the lemongrass, turmeric and peppercorns, adding 1–2 tablespoons of water if necessary to make a paste. Remove from the mortar and set aside.

To make the chilli paste, soak the dried chillies in warm water for about 10 minutes. Drain and place in the mortar. Pound into a smooth paste using the pestle. Add the shallot and shrimp paste and again pound into a fine paste.

Mix the tamarind pulp with 125 ml of warm water in a bowl and squeeze the pulp with your fingers to extract the juice. Strain the tamarind mix, discarding the pulp and seeds and reserving the tamarind water.

Heat a large saucepan over medium heat and add the coconut oil. Add the lemongrass paste and cook, stirring constantly, for 3–5 minutes, or until fragrant. Add the chilli paste and cook for 3 minutes, or until the oil separates from the spice paste and become red.

Add the tamarind juice to the pan, along with 500 ml of water. Bring to the boil, then add the mint and okra. Reduce the heat and simmer for 5 minutes. Add the fish heads and Asian greens, cover and simmer for 10 minutes, or until the fish is cooked. Season with salt to taste. Garnish with the ginger, coriander and mint and serve with cauliflower rice.

SERVES 4

TIP

To save yourself some time, you can use tamarind concentrate instead of tamarind pulp. Simply add 1 tablespoon of tamarind concentrate to the dish when you would normally add the tamarind water.

Have you ever noticed that kids seem to love food that is shaped into balls? I don't know why, but anything that gets them excited about eating is a good thing. Kids also love rolling these prawn cakes, so get them involved in the preparation. You can substitute the prawns with other types of seafood or use chicken. The lettuce cups are also a great way of getting raw veggies into your kids' systems.

PRAWN CAKES IN LETTUCE CUPS

600 g raw king prawns, shelled, deveined and diced

1 tablespoon fish sauce*

1 garlic clove, finely chopped

1 long red chilli, roughly chopped

1 spring onion, finely sliced

1 tablespoon ice-cold water

2 tablespoons sesame seeds

80 ml coconut oil, melted

sea salt and freshly ground black pepper

1 lime, halved

1 Lebanese cucumber, seeded and julienned

1 carrot, julienned

150 g bean sprouts

Vietnamese mint, Thai basil and coriander leaves, to serve

1 butter lettuce, leaves separated

LIME DIPPING SAUCE

1 small red chilli, roughly chopped

1 garlic clove, chopped

2 tablespoons fish sauce*

juice of 2 limes

* See Glossary

Process the prawns in a food processor until smooth and sticky. Add the fish sauce, garlic, chilli and spring onion and pulse to just combine. Add the water, then pulse to form a thick, coarse paste.

Brush your hands with oil so the prawn mixture won't stick to them, then divide the mixture into 10 equal portions and shape into golf-ball sized balls. Place the sesame seeds in a small bowl and roll the prawn cakes in them to coat.

Preheat a barbecue or chargrill pan to high and brush with the coconut oil. Cook the prawn cakes for 5 minutes, turning occasionally, until golden and cooked through. Sprinkle with a little salt and pepper, then squeeze over the juice from the lime halves.

To make the lime dipping sauce, pound the chilli and garlic with a mortar and pestle until almost smooth. Stir in the remaining ingredients and 3 tablespoons of water. Taste and adjust the flavours if necessary.

Place the prawn cakes, cucumber, carrot, bean sprouts, herbs and dipping sauce in small serving bowls. Arrange the lettuce cups on a platter, then allow your guests to fill their own lettuce cups with the prawn cakes, vegetables, herbs and dipping sauce.

SERVES 4

This refreshing dish has become somewhat of a staple in our household due to its incredible flavour and the fact that I can get it on the table within 15 minutes of assembling the ingredients. I highly recommend purchasing a mortar and pestle and some small airtight jars (or recycle pre-used ones). Fill the jars with a variety of freshly ground spices, label them and put them in an accessible spot so you remember to use them. Just a sprinkling of a few different types of spice can elevate a humble piece of fish, chicken or steak to mouth-watering levels. Now, I'm not usually one to use measurements as I love to experiment and create a different flavour every time, but this spice mix works a treat.

SPICED KINGFISH WITH AVOCADO TABOULEH

4 × 120 g kingfish fillets (or another firm white fish)

1 tablespoon coconut oil

lemon wedges, to serve (optional)

SPICE MIX

2 tablespoons cumin seeds

2 tablespoons fennel seeds

1 tablespoon coriander seeds

1 tablespoon sea salt

1 tablespoon freshly ground black pepper

SAUCE

80 g black tahini*

1 teaspoon harissa (for a recipe, see page 248) (optional)

1 tablespoon apple cider vinegar*

2 tablespoons extra-virgin olive oil

TABOULEH

50 g red quinoa*, rinsed

2 large handfuls of flat-leaf parsley leaves

2 large handfuls of coriander leaves

1 handful of mint leaves

2 tomatoes, finely chopped

½ Lebanese cucumber, diced

1 large avocado, diced

1 tablespoon sesame seeds, toasted

1 tablespoon lemon juice

* See Glossary

To make the spice mix, place all the spices in a spice grinder or mortar and pestle and grind to a fine powder. Mix in the salt and pepper.

To make the sauce, place all the ingredients in a bowl or a jar with a lid and mix or shake to combine. Add 2–4 tablespoons of water to thin the sauce a little.

To make the tabouleh, first cook the quinoa. Place it in a small saucepan with 160 ml of water and bring to the boil over high heat. Reduce the heat to low, cover and simmer for 10 minutes, or until all of the water is absorbed. Set aside to cool.

Finely chop the herbs and combine with the quinoa and other tablouleh ingredients in a small bowl.

Coat the fish in the spice mix. Melt the coconut oil in a frying pan over high heat and quickly sear the fish for 30 seconds on each side.

Place the tabouleh on serving plates, top with the fish and serve with the sauce and lemon wedges (if using).

SERVES 4

TIPS

I love to use fillets from the belly of the kingfish for this recipe.

Black tahini is made from black sesame seeds and is available from health food stores and Asian supermarkets.

I love to find healthy ways of reinventing family favourites. I make this dish about once a fortnight with fish, prawns or chicken, as it's so easy and so delicious. I get my daughters to help out with crumbing and they love it. The most important part of this dish is to get the freshest produce possible. It's great with sweet potato fries and, of course, a big salad of raw vegetables.

QUINOA-CRUMBED FISH

200 g quinoa flakes *

50 g shredded coconut

1 tablespoon finely chopped flat-leaf parsley leaves

2 tablespoons coconut flour

2 tablespoons buckwheat flour *

3 eggs, lightly whisked

600 g fish fillets, skinned and pin-boned (snapper, whiting and flathead are all great)

sea salt

150 ml coconut oil

lemon wedges, to serve

Sweet Potato Fries (page 162), to serve (optional)

aïoli (for a recipe, see page 252), to serve

mixed salad leaves, to serve

* See Glossary

Mix the quinoa flakes, shredded coconut and parsley in a shallow bowl. Mix the coconut flour and buckwheat flour in a second shallow bowl and the egg in another bowl.

Lightly season the fish with some salt, then dust with the flour mixture. Coat in the egg and roll in the crumbs, patting them on firmly.

Melt the coconut oil in a frying pan over medium heat and shallow-fry the fish for 1–2 minutes on each side, or until golden and crispy. Drain on paper towel.

Serve with the lemon wedges, sweet potato fries (if using), aïoli and salad leaves.

SERVES 4

TIP

Quinoa flakes are available at most health food stores. If you can't find any, you can substitute the same quantity of crushed macadamia nuts.

As you can tell, I am a huge fan of seafood. When the weather turns cool, I love big, hearty bowls of seafood curries, tagines and stews, and when the weather is warm, I can't go past light and refreshing seafood salads. This recipe combines the lightness of the watercress leaves with the earthiness of the root vegetables. Feel free to play around with different types of smoked seafood, or simply grill a piece of your favourite fish. As with all of my recipes, this is here for you to use as inspiration.

SMOKED OCEAN TROUT WITH BEETROOT AND HORSERADISH

8 small beetroot

1 celeriac, peeled and cut into thin batons

4 hard-boiled eggs, roughly chopped

8 cornichons, chopped

2 tablespoons chopped dill leaves, plus extra, to serve

2 tablespoons aïoli (for a recipe, see page 252)

sea salt and freshly ground black pepper

2 handfuls of watercress

1 tablespoon apple cider vinegar*

1 tablespoon lemon-infused extra-virgin olive oil

400 g lightly smoked fish (such as ocean trout, salmon, eel or kingfish), sliced

1 tablespoon grated horseradish*

1 tablespoon salmon roe

sunflower seeds, to serve

* See Glossary

Preheat the oven to 200°C.

Wrap the beetroot in foil and roast in the oven for 30–40 minutes, or until tender. Set aside to cool. When cool enough to handle, peel and cut in half.

Combine the celeriac, egg, cornichons and dill with the aïoli in a bowl and season with salt and pepper. Place in the middle of four serving plates.

Toss the beetroot and watercress with the vinegar and oil, season and arrange over the salad. To serve, top with the fish, horseradish, salmon roe, extra dill and sunflowers seeds.

SERVES 4

TIP

Lemon-infused extra-virgin olive oil can be found at delis and specialty food stores. If you can't find any, regular extra-virgin olive oil will be fine.

On one of my monthly visits to the fish markets, I came across the freshest sardines. Without a clue what I was going to make with them, I couldn't resist buying them on the spot. (Sardines contain high levels of omega-3, selenium, calcium, potassium, iron, vitamin B12 and vitamin D.) I typed 'sardine recipes' into a search engine on my phone – yes, even chefs need inspiration from time to time – and the one that stood out was a sour sardine curry. After a brief ponder, I remembered eating something similar in a fine Indian restaurant, so I thought, why not have a go at home? Wow, is all I can say! This recipe certainly packs a punch.

SOUR SARDINE CURRY

2 tablespoons coconut oil

12 curry leaves*

sea salt

4 Asian aubergines, chopped into large pieces

¼ cauliflower head (about 250 g), chopped into florets

16 okra*, cut into large pieces

20 whole sardines, cleaned

chopped coriander leaves, to garnish

MASALA PASTE

6 dried red chillies

8 black peppercorns

2 tablespoons coriander seeds

1 teaspoon yellow mustard seeds

1 teaspoon cumin seeds

1 teaspoon fenugreek seeds

1 small onion, chopped

2 teaspoons tamarind pulp*

* See Glossary

To make the masala paste, place all the ingredients except the onion and tamarind pulp in a large mortar and grind with a pestle until you have a fine powder. Add the onion and tamarind pulp and continue grinding until it becomes a paste. Transfer the paste to small bowl. Rinse the mortar with 800 ml of water and reserve the water.

Heat the oil in a large saucepan or wok over medium heat. Add the curry leaves and fry for a few seconds, or until fragrant. Add the masala paste and reserved masala water and season with salt. Add the aubergine, cauliflower and okra and bring to the boil.

One at a time, gently lower the sardines into the hot sauce. Cover and cook for 7–10 minutes, or until the sardines are just cooked. Taste for seasoning. Sprinkle over the chopped coriander and serve.

SERVES 4

TIP

Asian aubergines are longer and thinner than regular aubergines. They can be found at Asian grocers and some supermarkets. If you can't find any, regular aubergine will be fine.

This is an interpretation of the classic miso fish dish that has become synonymous with great Japanese restaurants the world over. The miso is usually mixed with large quantities of refined white sugar, which I have always struggled with. What are the alternatives? You can use honey or maple syrup (the real stuff), but I generally use brown rice syrup. The reason I love this recipe is that I like the idea of teaming fermented miso paste with a fermented rice product and a fermented soy sauce. There is so much research about the health benefits of fermented food. You will need to start this recipe the day before.

GRILLED FISH WITH MISO

2 tablespoons brown rice syrup* or honey

120 ml tamari*

250 ml white miso paste*

4 × 120 g barramundi fillets, skin left on

2 tablespoons coconut oil, melted

toasted black and white sesame seeds, to serve

lemon wedges, to serve

* See Glossary

Mix the brown rice syrup or honey, tamari and miso paste in a container (with a lid) and set aside.

Rinse the fish fillets and pat dry. Place the fish in the container, coat with marinade, cover and refrigerate overnight.

Preheat the oven to 170°C.

Remove the fish from the fridge and scrape off the marinade.

Brush an ovenproof chargrill or a frying pan with the coconut oil and place over high heat. Add the fish and cook for about 2 minutes on each side, or until browned. Transfer the fish to the oven and bake for about 8–10 minutes, or until nice and flaky.

Sprinkle with sesame seeds and serve with lemon wedges.

SERVES 4

These patties make a great go-to dish that is relatively inexpensive and satisfies everyone in family. I often just bake the whole mixture in the oven like a frittata. It is great to eat cold the next day, or you can pack any leftovers into lunchboxes. If you are following a paleo diet, you can omit the corn and quinoa.

TUNA AND SWEET POTATO PATTIES

80 g quinoa*, rinsed

480 g grated veggies (try parsnip, carrot, courgette, potato, pumpkin, Jerusalem artichoke)

½ small onion, grated

2 × 185 g cans tuna in olive oil or spring water

3–4 eggs

100 g corn kernels, cut from the cob

1 sweet potato (about 600 g), roasted and mashed

1 garlic clove, finely chopped

3 tablespoons chopped flat-leaf parsley leaves

2 tablespoons chia seeds*

2 handfuls of English spinach or Swiss chard, finely chopped

sea salt and freshly ground black pepper

coconut flour, to thicken, if needed

2 tablespoons coconut oil

1 lemon, cut into quarters, to serve

* See Glossary

Place the quinoa in a small saucepan with 160 ml of water and bring to the boil. Reduce the heat, cover and simmer for 15 minutes, or until the water is absorbed. Set aside to cool.

Place all the grated vegetables in a clean cloth or tea towel and squeeze out any excess liquid. Transfer to a bowl, add the quinoa, tuna, eggs, corn, sweet potato, garlic, parsley, chia seeds and spinach, season with salt and pepper and mix well. Add a little coconut flour if the mixture is too thin. Roll into small patties.

Heat the coconut oil in a large frying pan over medium heat and fry the patties for 2–4 minutes on each side, or until golden and crispy. Drain on paper towel, season with salt and pepper and serve with lemon wedges.

SERVES 6–8 AS A STARTER

Kids will love these patties, and you can add any grated vegetable you like to them.

It's common for people to be time-poor these days, so I appreciate the need
for convenience when it comes to food. I imagine most people would look at this recipe and
think, it's just not gonna happen. But I urge you to look at it with a different view –
that it provides not one, but two or three nutritious meals. With this tagine, I often make a
big pot full of the base (all the vegetables, herbs and spices), but before I add the seafood,
I will remove half or two-thirds of the mixture, allow it to cool and pop it in the fridge or
freezer. That way, the next time I want to make a tagine, I can just pull it out, reheat it and
add some fresh fish, mussels or prawns, or more veggies, like spinach, Swiss chard or kale.

FISH TAGINE WITH QUINOA AND GREEN OLIVES

6 baby beetroot, peeled

3 baby fennel bulbs, quartered

12 baby carrots

1 sweet potato, cut into wedges

10 okra*, halved lengthways

360 g chermoula (for a recipe, see page 246)

3 tablespoons honey

1½ teaspoons sea salt

60 g almonds (activated if possible, see page 176)

80 g green Sicilian olives

250 g red quinoa*, rinsed

600 g fish fillets, skinned, pin-boned and cut into 4 cm pieces (I love using cod, barramundi or snapper)

1 preserved lemon, skin rinsed and finely sliced

juice of 1½ lemons

coriander leaves, to serve

* See Glossary

Combine the beetroot, fennel, carrots, sweet potato, okra, chermoula, honey, salt, almonds and olives in a tagine or large saucepan with 1 litre of water and bring to the boil. Reduce the heat to low, cover and simmer for about 1 hour, or until the vegetables are well cooked.

While the vegetables are cooking, place the quinoa in a saucepan with 850 ml of water. Bring to the boil, then reduce heat, cover and cook for 15 minutes, or until all of the water is absorbed. Place the quinoa in a bowl or spread it on a tray and allow to cool.

Stir the fish and preserved lemon into the vegetables. Simmer, uncovered, for a few minutes, or until the fish is just cooked through, stirring very gently from time to time. Remove from the heat and stir in the lemon juice.

Scatter with coriander leaves and serve with the quinoa.

SERVES 4

I love a good feed of mussels, and it's not just because they taste delicious. Mussels are an affordable, environmentally sound, sustainable seafood, and gram for gram, fresh mussel meat, like many varieties of seafood, provides the same amount of high-quality protein as red meat, but with much less saturated fat and plenty of omega-3 fatty acids. Mussels are also an excellent source of iodine, iron, selenium, manganese and vitamin B12. I cook mussels at least once a week at home, whether it be a quick and simple mix of garlic, parsley and tomato or, if I've got more time up my sleeve, a sublime recipe like this Cambodian one.

CAMBODIAN MUSSELS

3 garlic cloves, peeled

1 small onion, roughly chopped

2 small green chillies, chopped

3 cm piece of fresh galangal*, peeled and roughly chopped

3 cm piece of ginger, peeled and roughly chopped

2 lemongrass stems, white part only, finely sliced

1 teaspoon finely sliced fresh turmeric or ½ teaspoon ground turmeric

2 tablespoons fish sauce*

300 g pumpkin, cut into 2 cm cubes

2 tablespoons coconut oil, melted

400 g can coconut milk

4 kaffir lime leaves*, torn

1 kg mussels, scrubbed and debearded

150 g Chinese broccoli (gai larn), chopped

150 g okra*, cut into 2 cm pieces

150 g Chinese cabbage (wong bok), chopped

juice of 1–2 limes

2 handfuls of coriander leaves, to serve

2 handfuls of Thai basil or Vietnamese mint leaves, to serve

* See Glossary

Preheat the oven to 180°C.

To make the paste, process the garlic, onion, chillies, galangal, ginger, lemongrass, turmeric, fish sauce and 2 tablespoons of water in a food processor until finely blended.

Coat the pumpkin in 1 tablespoon of the coconut oil, place on a baking tray and roast for 20–30 minutes, or until golden.

Heat the remaining coconut oil in a large saucepan or wok over medium–high heat. Add the paste and fry until aromatic, but do not allow it to colour as this may make the sauce bitter. Add the coconut milk and kaffir lime leaves and bring to the boil. Reduce the heat to a gentle simmer and cook for 10 minutes to allow the flavours to infuse and the liquid to reduce slightly.

Add the mussels, broccoli, okra and cabbage to the coconut milk mixture and simmer gently for 4–5 minutes, or until the mussels open. Stir through the lime juice and roasted pumpkin, then transfer to a large, shallow serving bowl. Serve immediately with the coriander and Thai basil or Vietnamese mint leaves.

SERVES 4

I'm fortunate to share a great friendship with an incredibly talented man, Gavin Baker. To say that he is the most inspirational chef I have ever met is an understatement. He's fearless in most areas of life, especially when it comes to cooking, and his deep understanding of how flavours work together blows my mind. We also share similar philosophies on life: the first being that we both wish to leave the world in a better state than when we entered it; the second that if you're going to eat, eat well and nourish your soul. I asked Gav to come up with a recipe for this book that was simple, used some stellar ingredients and would leave people wanting more. This is his creation from my brief. We both hope you love it.

PAN-FRIED WHITING WITH PUMPKIN AND KALE SALAD

600 g butternut pumpkin, cut into cubes

2 tablespoons coconut oil, melted

2 garlic cloves, crushed

sea salt

juice of ½ lemon

1 bunch of kale (about 400 g), central stalks removed and finely shredded

1 red Asian shallot, finely sliced

1 pomegranate, seeds only

finely grated zest of 1 lemon

4 whiting fillets, skin left on

freshly ground black pepper

MAPLE–MUSTARD DRESSING

3 tablespoons olive oil

1 tablespoon apple cider vinegar*

pinch of sea salt

1 tablespoon maple syrup

1 tablespoon Dijon mustard or Fermented Mustard (page 203)

* See Glossary

Preheat the oven to 200°C.

Toss the pumpkin with 1 tablespoon of the coconut oil, the garlic and a pinch of salt. Place on a lined baking tray and roast for 20–30 minutes, or until just tender but not mushy. Leave to cool for 5–10 minutes.

Meanwhile, combine the lemon juice and a pinch of salt in a large bowl and massage into the kale. Set aside for 20 minutes to allow the kale to wilt.

To make the dressing, whisk all the ingredients together in a bowl. Pour half of the dressing over the kale and toss to coat.

Add the pumpkin to the kale and toss together with the shallot, pomegranate seeds and lemon zest. Season to taste.

Season the whiting fillets with salt and pepper. Heat a frying pan over high heat and add the remaining tablespoon of coconut oil. Fry the whiting fillets for 2 minutes on each side, or until the skin is crispy and the fish is cooked.

Serve immediately with the pumpkin and kale salad and the remaining maple–mustard dressing.

SERVES 2

Oysters are often called nature's ultimate superfood – and rightfully so. They are one of the most nutrient-rich foods we can put into our bodies and also the most sustainable protein on the planet, actually helping to clean up our waterways. I am usually a purist when it comes to eating oysters – all I need is a good oyster knife and they are straight down the hatch. This recipe came about as I wanted to create a delicious way to eat oysters for breakfast. If oysters are not your cup of tea, this omelette will taste just as good with prawns, mussels, crab meat or even with just a few extra mushrooms.

OYSTER OMELETTE

4 dried shiitake mushrooms

2 tablespoons tamari *

4 cm piece of ginger, julienned

2 spring onions, finely sliced

2 handfuls of Asian greens, finely chopped

8 oysters, freshly shucked

6 eggs

2 teaspoons fish sauce *

large pinch of ground turmeric

2 teaspoons coconut oil

2 handfuls of bean sprouts

2 teaspoons sesame seeds, toasted

1 handful of snow pea sprouts

* See Glossary

Soak the mushrooms in 250 ml of boiling water for 5–10 minutes. Remove the mushrooms (reserving the water) and thinly slice.

Place the mushroom-soaking water and sliced mushrooms in a small saucepan with the tamari, ginger, spring onion and Asian greens. Add the oysters and gently poach for a few minutes over medium–low heat until they are warm. Remove from the heat. Use tongs to remove oysters and Asian greens, reserving the liquid.

Whisk the eggs, fish sauce and turmeric together in a bowl.

Heat 1 teaspoon of the coconut oil in a wok or frying pan over medium–high heat. Pour half the egg mixture into the wok and swirl to coat. Cook for 1 minute, then place half the oysters, Asian greens and bean sprouts on one side of the omelette. Cook for another 1–2 minutes, or until the egg is almost set, then flip the uncovered half of the omelette on top of the half with the oysters.

Slide the omelette onto a plate and keep warm. Repeat the above steps with the remaining coconut oil, egg mixture, oysters, Asian greens and bean sprouts to make a second omelette.

To serve, pour some of the oyster poaching liquid over the omelettes and scatter with the sesame seeds and snow pea sprouts.

SERVES 2

Chicken salad is one of those dishes that seems to bring a smile to everyone's face. It is easy, delicious and very good for you. I love taking inspiration from around the world, using spice rubs for the chicken or exotic dressings and sauces. Always use free-range, organic chicken, as it not only tastes better but is also better for you nutritionally. There are endless recipes for green goddess dressing and this is one of my all-time favourites. Please play around with it and create your own signature version!

CHICKEN SALAD with GREEN GODDESS DRESSING

2 large handfuls of cos lettuce leaves, torn

3 radishes, thinly sliced

1 handful of watercress

2 tablespoons walnut oil

sea salt and freshly ground black pepper

Green Goddess Dressing (page 251), to serve

2 skinless chicken breasts, cooked and thickly sliced

3 tablespoons chopped walnuts (activated if possible, see page 176)

zest of 1 lemon

To make the salad, gently wash and dry the cos lettuce. Combine the lettuce, radish and watercress in a bowl and gently mix with the walnut oil. Season with salt and pepper to taste.

Smear a generous amount of green goddess dressing onto two plates. Place the salad next to the dressing and arrange the chicken on top. Season with a little salt and pepper then scatter over the walnuts, lemon zest and a little more walnut oil if desired.

SERVES 2

I recently drove past a fast-food chicken outlet and couldn't believe the number of cars lined up outside. I wondered why people would wait in their cars for 10 minutes or more for chicken that was raised inhumanely and cooked in a way that research shows is harming us. It really doesn't take long to make it yourself, using ingredients that you can trust. I like to fry the chicken and then bake it in the oven to avoid an overcooked, bitter crust. Play around with different herbs, spices and cuisines – there is usually one form of fried chicken in most cultures. I am happy to share my recipe – no secret herbs and spices here!

SPICED CRISPY CHICKEN

4 eggs

2 tablespoons coconut milk

buckwheat flour*, for coating

1 × 1.8 kg chicken, cut into 10 pieces

coconut oil, for deep-frying

salad leaves, to serve

chopped almonds (activated if possible, see page 176), to serve

pumpkin seeds, to serve

lime wedges, to serve

aïoli (for a recipe, see page 252), to serve

SPICE MIX

200 g buckwheat flour*

1½ teaspoons dried oregano

1 teaspoon dried marjoram

2 teaspoons dried basil

1 teaspoon chilli powder

2 teaspoons freshly ground black pepper

2 teaspoons sea salt

1 teaspoon paprika

2 teaspoons ground cumin

1½ teaspoons garlic powder

1½ teaspoons onion powder

60 g quinoa flakes*

* See Glossary

Preheat the oven to 180°C.

First, make the spice mix by placing all the ingredients in a shallow bowl and mixing well.

Whisk the eggs and coconut milk in another shallow bowl. Place some buckwheat flour in a third shallow bowl, for coating the chicken.

Toss the chicken pieces in the buckwheat flour and dust off. Then dip them in the egg mix, followed by the spice mix, turning and pressing gently to coat thoroughly.

Add enough coconut oil to a large, heavy-based saucepan to bring it to one-third full. Place over medium–high heat until it reaches 170°C, or until a cube of bread dropped into the oil turns golden brown in 20 seconds.

Fry the chicken, in batches, for 3–6 minutes, or until golden. Transfer to a baking tray and roast 6–10 minutes, or until cooked through. Remove and drain on paper towel.

Serve with the salad leaves, almonds, pumpkin seeds, lime wedges and some aïoli for dipping.

SERVES 4

So much tastier, and healthier,
than the fast-food version!

Nonya cuisine is a blend of Chinese, Malay and other influences that combine to create the most sublime dishes featuring coconut, galangal, shrimp paste, tamarind, lemongrass and kaffir lime, to name just a few. When I visit Malaysia I am always astounded by how good the chicken curries are. One reason is that they sell the chickens live, so when you eat a chicken dish, there is a very good chance that the chook was alive only hours before. And then there are the spices that are so artfully woven into the dish, creating a magnificent depth of flavour. Water spinach is available at Asian grocers, but if you can't find any, you can use bok choy or choy sum instead.

NONYA CHICKEN CURRY

80 ml coconut oil

1 star anise

2 whole cloves

1 cinnamon stick

200 ml coconut cream

2 pandan leaves*, shredded lengthways and knotted (optional)

12 curry leaves*

600 g chicken thigh fillets, each fillet cut into 4 pieces

1 sweet potato (about 300 g), diced

150 g okra*, halved lengthways

400 ml coconut milk

1 tablespoon sea salt

2 small red chillies, halved lengthways and seeded (optional)

2 large handfuls of water spinach*

Cauliflower Rice (page 248), to serve

SPICE PASTE

8 dried red chillies

3 tablespoons coriander seeds

1 teaspoon cumin seeds

1 teaspoon fennel seeds

1 tablespoon shrimp paste (belacan)*

8–10 red Asian shallots (about 270 g), chopped

3 garlic cloves, chopped

6 cm piece of fresh turmeric root (about 25 g), chopped

* See Glossary

Start by making the spice paste. First, seed the chillies then place them in a small bowl and cover with boiling water. Soak for 10 minutes, then drain and chop.

Toast the coriander, cumin and fennel seeds in a dry frying pan over medium heat for 2 minutes, or until fragrant and beginning to smoke. Grind to a powder with a mortar and pestle or spice grinder and set aside.

Next, toast the shrimp paste in the same frying pan for 1–2 minutes, or until fragrant. Spoon into a small bowl and set aside.

The next step can be done the old-fashioned way or in a food processor. If using a mortar and pestle, pound the soaked chillies, adding a small amount at a time, until a fine paste forms. Continue to pound and add the ground spices, shrimp paste, shallots, garlic and turmeric until you have a smooth paste. If using a food processor, exercise the same patience and add only small amounts of the ingredients at a time.

Melt the coconut oil in a heavy-based saucepan or wok over medium heat. Fry the star anise, cloves and cinnamon stick for about 20 seconds, or until fragrant. Add the spice paste and sauté for 6–10 minutes, or until it is very fragrant and the oil starts to separate from the paste. Add 100 ml of the coconut cream, the pandan leaves (if using) and curry leaves and cook for a couple of minutes, or until the oil separates and rises to the surface. Stir in the chicken, sweet potato, okra, coconut milk and salt. Cover and simmer for 10–15 minutes, or until the chicken is cooked and the sweet potato tender. Add the remaining coconut cream and the chillies (if using) and simmer for a further 5 minutes. Remove from the heat and stir through the water spinach. Serve with cauliflower rice.

SERVES 4

Turkey is a wonderful source of protein and is slowly gaining popularity in Australia. It's low in saturated fat, has essential B vitamins and contains selenium, which is great for maintaining a healthy thyroid and immune system. And there's just no way that 300 million Americans can be wrong on Thanksgiving – turkey does indeed have a delicious flavour. I love this recipe as it's one the kids really enjoy and you can add as many grated veggies as you like – try carrot, parsnip, sweet potato and some thinly shredded kale.

TURKEY AND COURGETTE PATTIES

coconut oil, for cooking

4 handfuls of kale, chopped

juice of ½ lemon

1 fennel bulb, shaved

pinch of dried chilli flakes

sea salt and freshly ground black pepper

beetroot hummus (for a recipe, see page 186), to serve

Coconut Dressing (page 255), to serve (optional)

2 tablespoons toasted pine nuts, to serve

PATTIES

400 g turkey mince

1 large courgette (about 200 g), coarsely grated

3 spring onions, finely sliced

1 egg

2 tablespoons chopped mint leaves

2 tablespoons chopped coriander leaves

2 garlic cloves, crushed

1 teaspoon ground cumin

1 teaspoon sea salt

½ teaspoon coarsely ground black pepper

½ teaspoon cayenne pepper

Preheat the oven to 200°C. Line a tray with baking paper.

In a large bowl, mix all the ingredients for the patties. Shape into 18 small patties, each weighing about 45 g.

Add enough coconut oil to a large frying pan so that once it melts it is about 2 mm deep. Place over medium heat and sear the patties for about 2 minutes on each side, or until golden brown.

Carefully transfer the seared patties to a lined baking tray and place in the oven for 5–7 minutes, or until just cooked through.

Return the frying pan to medium heat and add a little more coconut oil if necessary. Add the kale and fry for 2–3 minutes, or until slightly wilted. Add the lemon juice, fennel and chilli flakes. Season with salt and pepper and remove from the heat.

To serve, place the kale on a plate then add the patties. Top with the beetroot hummus and coconut dressing (if using) and scatter over the pine nuts.

SERVES 4–6

TIPS

These patties can be made with other minced meats, like chicken, lamb, beef, prawn or fish. If the kids aren't too keen on beetroot hummus, then try aïoli (page 252) or cultured tomato ketchup (page 202).

Having witnessed first-hand the life that a factory-farmed chicken lives, I am happy to spend more on buying organic chicken. Chicken farmers have some of the worst farming practices that I have ever seen. These poor birds are pumped full of hormones and antibiotics, and endure extremely high stress levels throughout their short lives. If you aren't already buying organic chicken, I urge you to do some research before you buy your next bird, and support the farmers who are ethically raising chooks. This is a lovely, lightly spiced chicken recipe that's perfect for any time of the year. You will need to start it the day before.

LEBANESE CHICKEN WITH RADISH SALAD

1 kg butterflied chicken pieces (ask your butcher to do this)

sea salt and freshly ground black pepper

MARINADE

1 tablespoon ground cinnamon

2 tablespoons ground cumin

10 cardamom pods

4 allspice berries

1 tablespoon ground turmeric

1½ teaspoons paprika

4 garlic cloves, chopped

3–5 cm piece of ginger (about 30 g), peeled and coarsely chopped

2 tablespoons honey

180 ml olive oil

SALAD

1 long red chilli, seeded and sliced

1 spring onion, finely sliced

3 radishes, finely sliced

1 Lebanese cucumber, diced

5 okra*, sliced

1 lemon, segmented (see tip)

2 tablespoons extra-virgin olive oil

1 tablespoon apple cider vinegar*

3 tablespoons chopped flat-leaf parsley leaves

3 tablespoons chopped coriander leaves

3 tablespoons chopped mint leaves

* See Glossary

Start by making the marinade. Put all the spices in a food processor or spice grinder and process until you have a fine powder. Add the garlic and ginger and process to a paste. Transfer to a bowl and whisk in the honey and oil.

Rub the marinade into the skin and flesh of the chicken. Cover and chill for at least 4 hours, preferably overnight.

Remove the chicken from the fridge and season with a little salt and pepper.

Heat a barbecue to high or preheat the oven to 180°C. If you are using a barbecue, cook the chicken for 10–14 minutes, or until cooked through, turning over after 5–7 minutes. Alternatively, place it on a baking tray, spaced well apart, and roast in the oven for about 20 minutes, or until cooked through.

To make the salad, combine the chilli, spring onion, radish, cucumber, okra and lemon in a bowl. Add the oil, vinegar and herbs, season to taste and gently toss.

Serve the chicken with the radish salad.

SERVES 4

TIP

To segment a lemon, first remove the zest and white pith. Use a small, sharp knife to cut alongside the membrane of one segment to the centre of the lemon. Cut along the other side of the segment and you should be able to remove the segment. Repeat this process for the remaining segments.

There are many variations of this fabulous classic. The chicken can be steamed, boiled, poached, grilled, fried or barbecued. And you don't necessarily have to use chicken – you can try roasted duck, thinly sliced seared beef, minced lamb, or seafood, such as freshly picked crab meat or cooked prawns, even canned tuna or raw fish. The main thing to remember is to use loads of fresh herbs to add as much flavour as possible. And, of course, the dressing is crucial, too. I like my dressing to be salty, sour and hot, which is achieved through the use of fish sauce, chilli and lime juice.

VIETNAMESE CHICKEN SALAD

½ small Chinese cabbage (about 300 g), shredded

2 large handfuls of coriander leaves

1 handful of mint leaves

1 handful of Thai basil leaves

½ carrot, julienned

3 tablespoons fried shallots (for a recipe, see page 252)

2 tablespoons fried garlic (for a recipe, see page 252)

80 g almonds (activated if possible, see page 176), crushed

PICKLED SHALLOTS

2 red Asian shallots

3 tablespoons apple cider vinegar*

MARINATED CHICKEN

1 kg chicken marylands

1 tablespoon finely grated ginger

2 large garlic cloves, crushed

3 tablespoons fish sauce*

3 tablespoons coconut oil, melted

salt and freshly ground black pepper

FISH SAUCE DRESSING

170 ml fish sauce*

2 tablespoons honey

2 tablespoons finely grated ginger

3 garlic cloves, crushed

1–2 long red chillies, finely chopped

3–4 tablespoons lime juice

* *See Glossary*

Preheat the oven to 200°C.

To pickle the shallots, place the shallots and vinegar in a bowl and let sit for 20 minutes, then drain.

To marinate the chicken, place the chicken, ginger, garlic, fish sauce and 2 tablespoons of the coconut oil in a bowl and mix well. Set aside for about 20 minutes.

Place the marinated chicken on a baking tray and rub with the remaining tablespoon of coconut oil. Season with salt and pepper and bake for 20 minutes, or until cooked through. Remove from the oven and set aside to cool.

Once the chicken is cool enough to handle, shred the meat by hand.

Next, make the fish sauce dressing. In a bowl or large jar, combine all the ingredients with 80 ml of water. Taste and add a little more lime juice if necessary.

Combine the cabbage, herbs and carrot in a large bowl and toss well.

To serve, toss the chicken and enough dressing to taste through the salad. Top with the fried shallots, fried garlic, almonds and pickled shallots.

SERVES 4

TIP

You can keep any leftover fish sauce dressing in an airtight jar in the fridge for up to 1 month.

I love travelling to South-East Asia. Not only are its cultures diverse and unique, but it is a gourmet paradise of exciting and eye-opening produce, flavours and aromas. Spiced fish in banana leaves, or otak-otak, is one dish that is very popular in a lot of South-East Asian countries. You can see it being cooked everywhere, from little market stalls to high-end restaurants. It is relatively easy to make at home and always impresses at a dinner party. You can make this dish with minced prawns or fish instead of chicken.

SPICED CHICKEN IN BANANA LEAVES

4–6 red Asian shallots (about 150 g), peeled and chopped

4 macadamia nuts

5 kaffir lime leaves*, finely sliced

1 lemongrass stem, white part only, sliced as finely as possible

3 garlic cloves, peeled

2 teaspoons shrimp paste (belacan)*

2.5 cm piece of fresh galangal*, sliced

3 dried red chillies

2 tablespoons coconut oil

2 eggs

½ teaspoon curry powder

½ teaspoon ground turmeric

125 ml coconut cream or milk

2 tablespoons fish sauce*

1–2 tablespoons coconut flour

600 g chicken mince

sea salt and freshly ground black pepper

4 large banana leaves

dried chilli flakes, to serve

coriander leaves, to serve

lime halves, to serve

* See Glossary

Combine the shallots, macadamia nuts, kaffir lime leaves, lemongrass, garlic, shrimp paste, galangal, dried chilli and oil in a food processor and process to a smooth paste.

Transfer the paste to a bowl and add the eggs, curry powder, turmeric, coconut cream or milk, fish sauce and 1 tablespoon of the coconut flour. Mix well, adding a little more flour if the mixture is too wet (it should be similar in consistency to a burger patty mix). Stir through the chicken mince and season with salt and pepper.

Soak the banana leaves in hot water for 5–10 minutes, or until softened. Wipe the leaves dry with paper towel and cut into 16 pieces, each measuring 20 cm × 10 cm. The longer length must run parallel to the lines of the banana leaf.

Place about 3 tablespoons of chicken paste in the centre of each piece of banana leaf. Gently squeeze the edges of the banana leaves to form a bow-tie shape. You must fold along the lines of the banana leaf and not against, or the banana leaf will crack and break. Use bamboo toothpicks or a piece of kitchen string to secure both ends of the otak-otak. Repeat until all the banana leaf pieces and paste are used up.

Line the base of a large steamer with baking paper. Place the banana leaf parcels inside in a single layer. Pour water into a wok or large saucepan until one-quarter full and bring to the boil over high heat. Place the steamer over the wok, ensuring the base doesn't touch the water. Steam for 10–12 minutes, or until cooked through.

Scatter with chilli flakes and coriander and serve with lime halves.

MAKES 16

I visited an Aboriginal community a few years back and they wanted to share with me one of their traditional foods – turtle. I watched the slaughter of this beautiful creature and, although it was rather gruesome, the thing that stood out was how the whole community got involved. Everyone had a job to do, from cleaning the intestines to preparing the organ meat, and I noticed how the offal was the most sought-after part of the turtle. Offal has the highest nutritional value of any the part of an animal and yet, sadly, we rarely cook with it. I have included this recipe as it is so moreish yet isn't heavily laden with butter, as most pâtés are.

SIMPLE CHICKEN LIVER PÂTÉ

1 tablespoon coconut oil

1 onion, finely diced

1 celery stalk, finely diced

1 carrot, finely diced

4 garlic cloves, finely chopped

2 tablespoons chopped thyme leaves (or any other herbs, such as sage or rosemary)

1 kg chicken livers, trimmed of sinew

2 teaspoons sea salt

1 tablespoon freshly ground black pepper

1 tablespoon pau d'arco powder* (optional)

1½ teaspoons licorice root powder* (optional)

1 teaspoon slippery elm powder* (optional)

300 ml coconut oil, melted

extra melted coconut oil, for storing

Seed Crackers (page 179), to serve

Cultured Beetroot, Apple and Carrot (page 207), to serve

coriander leaves, to serve

* See Glossary

Place the coconut oil in a large saucepan with the onion, celery, carrot, garlic and thyme. Cook over low heat until the onion is soft and transparent. Add the chicken livers, salt, pepper, as well as the pau d'arco powder, licorice root powder and slippery elm powder (if using). Add 250 ml of water to the pan, then cover and cook, stirring occasionally, over low heat for 5–8 minutes, or until the livers are medium–rare. Remove from the heat and set aside to cool.

Once cool, place half the liver mix in a food processor and process until smooth, using a spatula to scrape the mixture from the sides. Slowly pour in 150 ml of the melted coconut oil while the motor is running and process until well combined. Adjust the seasoning then transfer the pâté to a bowl and repeat the above steps with the remaining liver mix and coconut oil.

Pass the pâté through a fine sieve, then pour into jars, ceramic bowls or small dishes. Pour a small amount of coconut oil evenly over the surface of the pâté, so that it is entirely covered.

Cover with plastic wrap and place in the fridge overnight to set. Store in the fridge for up to 4 days, or in the freezer for up to 3 months. Serve with seed crackers, cultured beetroot, apple and carrot, and coriander leaves.

SERVES 8 AS A STARTER

TIP

Adding coconut oil to seal the top of the pâté prevents it from discolouring due to oxidation and allows you to store it for longer in the fridge.

Roast chook would have to be the ultimate comfort food. I like to take culinary inspiration from around the globe and turn a simple roast chicken into something memorable. This Chinese-inspired recipe is a new favourite. The highlights are the vinegar in the sauce and the wonderful healing aromatics of garlic, ginger and chilli. For maximum flavour, start this recipe the day before.

SHANTUNG ROAST CHICKEN

1 × 1.2 kg chicken

steamed Asian greens, such as Chinese broccoli or bok choy, to serve

Cucumber Salad with Avocado and Ginger (page 68), to serve (optional)

MARINADE

4 garlic cloves, chopped

3 tablespoons finely grated ginger

1 long red chilli, chopped

1 tablespoon chopped coriander roots and stems

2 teaspoons Sichuan peppercorns*

80 ml tamari*

80 ml shaoxing rice wine*

2 tablespoons coconut oil

SAUCE

1 tablespoon honey

2 tablespoons tamari*

2 tablespoons apple cider vinegar* or Chinese black vinegar

2 garlic cloves, finely chopped

1 long red chilli, thinly sliced

few drops of sesame oil

1 tablespoon toasted sesame seeds

1 handful of coriander leaves, chopped

* See Glossary

To make the marinade, process or pound the garlic, ginger, chilli, coriander roots and stems and Sichuan peppercorns in a food processor or with a mortar and pestle until they form a paste. Add the tamari, rice wine and oil and mix until well combined.

Place the chicken in a large bowl and pour over the marinade, rubbing it into the chicken well. Place the chicken in the fridge to marinate for at least an hour, or ideally overnight.

Preheat the oven to 180°C.

Place the marinated chicken on a sheet of foil, wrap up and place on a baking tray. Roast for 1¼ hours, then remove the foil and roast for a further 20 minutes, or until the chicken is cooked and the skin is golden brown. Remove from the oven and rest in a warm place for 20 minutes.

To make the sauce, mix all the ingredients in a bowl.

Serve the chicken with the sauce, a big platter of steamed Asian greens and cucumber salad (if using).

SERVES 4

Spice up an ordinary roast chicken with this marinade of tamari, garlic, ginger and Sichuan peppercorns.

This is a Laotian classic that traditionally features ground toasted rice as its textural component. I've played around with it and found that toasted quinoa works just as well, if not better. You can use any mince for this recipe – pork, beef, duck, prawn – and it will be delicious, but chicken is cheaper and more readily available. I like to use organic chicken at home and this is a great way of eating organic without breaking the bank.

LAOTIAN CHICKEN SALAD *WITH* TOASTED QUINOA

80 g quinoa*

1 tablespoon coconut oil

500 g chicken mince

80 ml lime juice

2 tablespoons fish sauce*

1 garlic clove, finely chopped

1 small red chilli, halved, seeded and sliced

½ small red onion, finely diced

1 handful of Thai basil leaves, torn

1 large handful of coriander leaves, torn

1 handful of Vietnamese mint leaves, torn

1 large handful of mint leaves, torn

6 spring onions, green part only, finely sliced

1 Lebanese cucumber, finely diced

120 g green beans, finely sliced

sea salt and freshly ground black pepper

8 red cabbage leaves

* See Glossary

Heat a wok or frying pan over medium–high heat. Add the quinoa and cook, shaking the pan constantly, for 2–3 minutes, or until the quinoa is golden and toasted. Remove from the pan and spread out on a tray to cool completely.

Wipe the wok or pan clean and place over medium–high heat. Add the coconut oil and chicken mince and stir-fry for 2–3 minutes, or until the chicken is cooked and crumbly. Stir in the lime juice, fish sauce, garlic, chilli and onion, then remove from the heat and allow to cool.

When you are ready to serve, add the herbs, spring onion, cucumber, green beans and toasted quinoa to the chicken and mix well to combine. Taste and adjust the seasoning. Spoon the salad into red cabbage leaves and serve.

SERVES 4

Raw meat dishes are some of my favourites because they're nutritious, delicious and so easy to make. Our eating habits have changed from those of our primal ancestors who, just like every other carnivore on the planet, chose to consume their kill raw. Eventually, humans evolved, learned to control fire and began cooking their food. However, many cultures around the world still consume raw meat in one form or another. This dish is a variation of the musk ox tartare I learnt from Noma's Rene Redzepi when I had the good fortune to work alongside him years ago.

BEEF CARPACCIO WITH TARRAGON

2 French shallots, finely sliced

80 ml apple cider vinegar*

400 g beef eye fillet, minced

1 large handful of watercress leaves, to serve

1 tablespoon grated horseradish*, to serve

SPICE MIX

1 tablespoon juniper berries*

½ tablespoon coriander seeds

½ tablespoon caraway seeds

1 teaspoon ground cumin

1 tablespoon sea salt

½ tablespoon black peppercorns

TARRAGON SAUCE

1 small handful of tarragon leaves

100 ml chicken stock (for a recipe, see page 38)

2½ tablespoons apple cider vinegar*

1 French shallot, peeled

¼ garlic clove, peeled

1 teaspoon chia seeds*

* See Glossary

To make the spice mix, toast all the ingredients in a dry frying pan for 2 minutes, or until fragrant. Grind to a fine powder in a spice grinder or using a mortar and pestle. Set aside.

Place the shallots in the apple cider vinegar to pickle for 5–10 minutes. Drain, then set aside.

Divide the mince into four equal portions. Place each mound in the middle of a large sheet of plastic wrap. Place another sheet of plastic wrap on top, then gently and evenly roll out with a rolling pin until the meat is 2 mm thick. Repeat this process with the remaining portions of mince. Transfer the meat to a tray then place in the freezer for 10–15 minutes, or until it is partly frozen.

While the meat is in the freezer, make the tarragon sauce. Place all the ingredients in a food processor and process until smooth. Season to taste, then transfer to a small jug.

When the meat is ready, remove the top sheet of plastic wrap and invert onto a serving plate, then remove the remaining piece of plastic wrap. Repeat for the remaining portions of meat.

To serve, sprinkle with the spice mix and drizzle on the sauce. Top with the watercress, horseradish and pickled shallots.

SERVES 4

TIPS

Make sure the animal you use for this dish has been humanely raised and grass fed by a reputable farmer in order to minimise the risk of bacteria and parasites. It's also a good idea to freeze and thaw the meat prior to preparing. And it's got to be said, it's always wise to check with your health adviser before consuming raw meat.

Chimichurri is an Argentinean sauce used for grilled meats, and it is my absolute favourite at the moment. The ingredients alone from a health point of view are astounding: garlic, parsley, coriander, apple cider vinegar and coconut oil. You can use chimichurri as a sauce or condiment, as a marinade for meat, chicken or seafood, or you can thin it down with a little water to make a beautiful salad dressing. Chimichurri is also delicious with sweet potato, pumpkin and plenty of other vegetables.

CHIMICHURRI BEEF HEART SKEWERS

1.5–2 kg grass-fed beef heart

coconut oil, for cooking

sea salt and freshly ground
black pepper

dried chilli flakes, to serve

CHIMICHURRI
6 garlic cloves, peeled

sea salt

2 jalapeno chillies, chopped

2 very large handfuls of flat-leaf
parsley leaves

2 very large handfuls of coriander
leaves

200 ml apple cider vinegar *

pinch of ground cumin

300 ml coconut oil, melted

freshly ground black pepper

* See Glossary

Soak 8 bamboo skewers in warm water for 20 minutes before using, or use metal skewers.

Cut all the fat, vessels, veins and sinew off the beef heart, then cut into 3 cm cubes. Thread 3–4 cubes onto each skewer and set aside on a tray.

To make the sauce, place the garlic and a little salt in a mortar and crush with the pestle. Add the chilli, parsley and coriander and pound to a paste. Stir through the vinegar, cumin and coconut oil, then taste and season with salt and pepper.

Pour half the sauce over the skewers, cover and place in the fridge to marinate for at least 2 hours, or ideally overnight. Place the remaining sauce in the fridge.

When you are ready to serve, heat a barbecue to medium–high and grease with a little coconut oil. Season the skewers with salt and pepper and cook for 2 minutes on each side, or until cooked to your liking. Remove from the heat and leave to rest in a warm place for 5 minutes.

Sprinkle with the chilli flakes and serve with the remaining chimichurri.

SERVES 4 AS A STARTER

TIP

I make this dish with beef heart, as it is especially dense with nutrients and I like the flavour. However, you can easily substitute beef fillet, chicken or fish if you are not keen on beef heart.

Cinnamon is one of the oldest known spices. It's a favourite in my house because it's delicious and has some great health benenfits. It stimulates circulation, is good for digestion and helps to settle upset stomachs. Its mildness means that it's a spice kids can enjoy. This is a lovely recipe for cooler months, when it's comforting to stock up on nourishing meals that warm our souls. I have teamed this delicious stew with gremolata – an Italian preparation of chopped parsley, lemon zest and garlic.

CINNAMON-BRAISED SHORT RIBS WITH PUMPKIN

2 tablespoons coconut oil

1 kg beef short ribs, bone in

100 g spring onion, chopped

2 large carrots, roughly chopped

2 garlic cloves, crushed

400 g can chopped tomatoes

5 thyme sprigs

2 rosemary sprigs

500 ml beef stock (for a recipe, see page 39)

zest of ½ orange, peeled off in long strips

1 bay leaf

2 cinnamon sticks

1 star anise

2 teaspoons licorice root powder *

½ teaspoon freshly ground black pepper

sea salt

300 g butternut pumpkin, cut into 2.5 cm cubes

100 g Swiss chard

3 tablespoons toasted, chopped hazelnuts

GREMOLATA

2 tablespoons roughly chopped flat-leaf parsley leaves

finely grated zest of 1 large lemon

2 garlic cloves, crushed

* See Glossary

Preheat the oven to 170°C.

Place a large, heavy-based, flameproof casserole dish over high heat and add the coconut oil. When this is smoking hot, add some of the beef ribs and sear on all sides, browning well, for about 4 minutes. (Make sure you don't cook too many pieces at once or they will boil in their own liquid rather than fry.) Transfer the beef ribs to a colander to drain the excess fat while you brown the remaining pieces.

Remove most of the fat from the dish and add the spring onion, carrot and garlic. Place over medium–high heat and sauté, stirring occasionally, for about 10 minutes, or until the vegetables are golden brown. Stir in the tomatoes. Tie the thyme and rosemary sprigs together with kitchen string and drop in as well, then add the stock, orange zest, bay leaf, cinnamon sticks, star anise, licorice root powder, pepper and some salt.

Place the ribs on the sauce in one layer. Cover first with a sheet of baking paper, then with a tight-fitting lid or a couple of layers of foil. Transfer to the oven and bake for 2–3 hours, or until the meat falls off the bone. Add more water during the cooking process if it starts to look too dry. Lift the ribs from the sauce, place in a large bowl and leave to cool slightly.

Add the pumpkin and 300 ml of water to the sauce and bring to the boil on the stovetop. Reduce the heat to low and simmer gently for 30 minutes, or until the pumpkin is soft. Stir through the Swiss chard and hazelnuts and cook for about 5 minutes, or until the Swiss chard is just tender. Return the ribs to the sauce for 1–2 minutes, or until warmed through. Taste and season with more salt and pepper.

To make the gremolata, simply mix the parsley, lemon zest and garlic together. Transfer the ribs and sauce to a serving bowl and scatter a little gremolata on top.

SERVES 4

Kangaroo is delicious, native, abundant and extremely healthy, with a low fat content and lots of iron. In this recipe I have teamed roo with Moroccan flavours, as I love the intoxicating aroma that fills the kitchen when cooking with spices like this. If you can't find roo mince, use kangaroo fillet instead – just cut it into strips and thread it onto skewers. You could also substitute lamb, beef or emu mince. Our kids absolutely love this dish and aren't opposed to eating emu or kangaroo at all.

MOROCCAN SPICED KANGAROO MEATBALLS

400 g kangaroo mince

1 garlic clove, finely chopped

1 tomato, seeded and finely diced

sea salt and freshly ground black pepper

coconut oil, for cooking

1 teaspoon pomegranate molasses*, plus extra, to serve

seeds of 1 pomegranate, to serve

1 handful of mint leaves, chopped, to serve

MOROCCAN SPICE MIX

4 tablespoons ground cumin

3 tablespoons dried mint

3 tablespoons dried oregano

2 tablespoons sweet paprika

2 tablespoons freshly ground black pepper

2 teaspoons hot paprika

POMEGRANATE SAUCE

125 ml unhulled tahini*

1 tablespoon lemon juice

1 tablespoon pomegranate molasses*

½ teaspoon ground cumin

1 small handful of mint leaves, chopped

1 teaspoon sumac*

* See Glossary

To make the Moroccan spice mix, place all the ingredients in an airtight container and shake to combine.

Place the kangaroo mince, garlic, tomato and 2 ½ tablespoons of the spice mix in a bowl. Mix thoroughly and season with salt and pepper. Divide into eight portions and shape into balls. Refrigerate for 30 minutes to set before cooking.

To make the pomegranate sauce, place all the ingredients in a bowl with 125 ml of water and stir until smooth. Add a little more water if necessary to reach sauce consistency.

Preheat a barbecue hotplate to medium and grease with a little coconut oil. Cook the kangaroo balls for about 6 minutes, rolling them around to make sure they cook evenly on all sides.

To serve, place the kangaroo balls on a plate, drizzle with the pomegranate molasses and scatter over the pomegranate seeds and mint. Serve the pomegranate sauce on the side, along with skewers or toothpicks to help people pick up the balls.

SERVES 4 AS A STARTER

TIP

You can keep any remaining Moroccan spice mix in an airtight container for up to a month.

In many households, Thai beef salad would have to be a firm favourite. It's so simple to prepare. You just briefly sear the meat, slice it, assemble the other ingredients (my kids love to pick the herbs and it's a great way to teach them to identify herbs by look, taste and smell) and whiz together a quick dressing. Most Thai beef salads include rice noodles, but I prefer kelp noodles as they contain calcium, iodine, magnesium, potassium and other essential minerals. If you can't find kelp noodles, use slow-roasted sweet potato or pumpkin instead. As always, search out the best pasture-raised beef.

THAI BEEF SALAD

400 g kelp noodles*

3 tablespoons sea salt

3 tablespoons freshly ground black pepper

1 × 600 g piece of eye fillet

2 tablespoons coconut oil

3 spring onions, finely sliced on the diagonal

1 small handful of Thai basil leaves

1 small handful of mint leaves

1 small handful of coriander leaves

2 tablespoons chopped almonds (activated if possible, see page 176)

DRESSING

2 tablespoons finely diced ginger

2 tablespoons finely chopped coriander stems

3 garlic cloves, finely chopped

1 long red chilli, finely sliced

1 tablespoon honey (optional)

2 tablespoons apple cider vinegar*

2 tablespoons tamari*

1 tablespoon finely chopped lemongrass, white part only

1 teaspoon sesame oil

3 tablespoons extra-virgin olive oil

* See Glossary

Soak the kelp noodles in a bowl of warm water for 20–30 minutes to slightly soften. Drain and set aside.

Heat the barbecue or grill to high. Put the salt and pepper on a tray and evenly roll the eye fillet in it. Lightly brush the barbecue or grill with the coconut oil and sear the beef for 4–5 minutes on each side. Rest for 10 minutes before slicing (or place in the fridge to cool before slicing).

To make the dressing, combine the ginger, coriander, garlic, chilli, honey (if using), vinegar, tamari, lemongrass, sesame oil and olive oil in a bowl and mix well.

Pour half the dressing over the noodles and gently toss.

To serve, arrange the noodles on a platter and top with the beef slices, spring onion and herbs, the remaining dressing and the nuts. Toss to combine. You can serve this dish at room temperature or chilled.

SERVES 4

TIP

Substitute the beef for prawns, leftover poached or roasted chicken, tuna sashimi or canned tuna (responsibly fished).

You may be shocked to find a burger in a health-oriented cookbook, but the truth is you can easily create a burger that will satisfy your tastebuds and nourish your body, too. Let's begin by looking at a normal fast-food burger. Do they use grass-fed, humanely raised animals? Does the bun have any nutritional value at all? Is the tomato sauce free of sugar and made from organic tomatoes? And is the cheese made from a healthy cow's milk? The answer to all of these questions is probably a firm 'NO!' But what if we used grass-fed meat from a cow that has had a stress-free life, left out the bread altogether, used tomato sauce that is homemade and sugar free, and added lots of fresh nutritious ingredients that complement the patty and sauce? YUM!

BURGER with THE LOT

2 tablespoons coconut oil

2 onions, cut into thick slices

80 ml Cultured Tomato Ketchup (page 202)

2 tablespoons Fermented Mustard (page 203)

80 ml aïoli (for a recipe, see page 252)

12 slices of tomato

8 slices of gherkin

1 avocado, sliced

2 large handfuls of rocket

4 tablespoons Cultured Beetroot, Apple and Carrot (page 207)

PATTIES

600 g chuck steak, minced

2 garlic cloves, crushed

pinch of dried chilli flakes

2 tablespoons chopped flat-leaf parsley leaves

pinch of dried oregano

1 egg

1 teaspoon sea salt

1 teaspoon freshly ground black pepper

½ onion, finely diced

1 tablespoon Dijon or wholegrain mustard

SWEET POTATO FRIES

coconut oil, for greasing

800g sweet potato

80 ml coconut oil, melted

½ teaspoon sea salt

½ teaspoon pepper

3 rosemary sprigs, leaves picked and roughly chopped

10 sage leaves, roughly chopped

To make the patties, mix all the ingredients in a large bowl. Shape into four patties and refrigerate until ready to cook.

To make the sweet potato fries, preheat the oven to 220°C and lightly grease a large baking tray with coconut oil. Cut the sweet potato into 5 mm thick slices, then cut these into 5 mm thick batons. Place the sweet potato, melted coconut oil, salt, pepper, rosemary and sage in a large bowl and mix well. Spread on the prepared tray in a single layer. Bake for 10 minutes, then turn the fries over and continue baking for another 5 minutes, or until tender and lightly browned. Keep a close eye on the fries as they can burn easily.

Heat a barbecue or grill to medium–high and add the coconut oil. Place the onion and patties on the barbecue. Cook for 5 minutes, then turn the patties over and continue cooking both the onions and patties for a couple of minutes, or until just done.

Place the patties in the middle of the table with all of the other toppings and extras in bowls and let everyone help themselves.

SERVES 4

MEAT

These burgers look great when plated up with all the sides, but if you don't have the time, simply place all the sides in bowls on the table and let people help themselves.

I couldn't live without spices. Their health benefits are an added bonus to the tantalising tastes they create when used in cooking. I buy my mince from our organic butcher because it has a good quantity of fat and they use all the parts of the animal when they make it, which I love. This simple recipe can be used to make meatballs, patties or sausages. Feel free to serve them with some tahini or yoghurt.

MIDDLE EASTERN SAUSAGES WITH CORIANDER SAUCE

600 g beef mince

2 large handfuls of coriander leaves and stems, finely chopped

1 large handful of mint leaves, finely chopped

1 onion, finely chopped

2 teaspoons ground coriander

½ teaspoon ground turmeric

1 teaspoon grated ginger

1 teaspoon ground cumin

juice of ½ lime

2 eggs

1 tablespoon tomato paste

1 long green chilli, finely diced

2 tablespoons coconut oil

1 teaspoon sea salt

chopped tomatoes, to serve

coriander leaves, to serve

CORIANDER SAUCE

3 large handfuls of coriander leaves and stems, chopped

2 handfuls of mint leaves, chopped

1 teaspoon sea salt

juice of ½ lime

1 small red chilli, halved, seeded and sliced

3 tablespoons coconut oil

1 tablespoon ground fenugreek (optional)

Soak 8 bamboo skewers in water for 20 minutes, or use metal skewers.

To make the sausages, place all the ingredients except the tomatoes in a large bowl and mix well. Shape the mixture into small sausage shapes around the skewers. Place on a tray, cover with plastic wrap and allow to rest in the fridge for at least 1 hour.

Meanwhile, to make the sauce, put the coriander, mint, salt, lime juice, chilli and coconut oil in a blender. Add up to 3 tablespoons of water – you want to just moisten the mixture – then blend to make a sauce. If it's too thin or watery, add the fenugreek to thicken. Transfer to a bowl, cover and set aside.

When you are ready to cook, heat the barbecue or grill to low–medium and cook the skewers, turning frequently, for 10 minutes, or until cooked through and nicely browned.

Serve with the coriander sauce, tomatoes and coriander leaves.

SERVES 4 AS A STARTER

During the warmer months, I generally eat cool foods, like seafood and salads, and once the chill returns, warming stews, soups and curries nourish me. Choosing your style of dish with the weather in mind makes a lot of sense. Lamb osso buco has always been a favourite during the winter months. I vividly remember making osso buco by the thousands in my early days as an apprentice chef at an Italian restaurant. I actually bumped into Russell Gronow, my executive chef from 25 years ago, the other day, and asked him if I could put his osso buco recipe in this book. Thanks for everything, Russell; you taught me great respect for the craft of cooking.

LAMB OSSO BUCO

2 litres beef stock (for a recipe, see page 39)

3 ½ tablespoons coconut oil

1 kg lamb shanks, cut in half (ask your butcher to do this)

4 garlic cloves, crushed

1 onion, finely sliced

6 rosemary sprigs, leaves picked and roughly chopped

1 long red chilli, split lengthways

sea salt

1 carrot, roughly diced

2 celery stalks, roughly diced

2 tablespoons tomato paste

300 g canned whole peeled tomatoes

¼ cauliflower head (about 250 g), chopped into small florets

¼ bunch of cavolo nero (about 300 g), roughly shredded

freshly ground black pepper

Preheat the oven to 160°C.

Pour the beef stock into a large saucepan and bring to the boil over medium–high heat. Continue to cook until the stock has reduced by half and is now 1 litre (this should take 15–20 minutes). Using this reduced stock will make the final dish richer and more delicious.

Place a frying pan over medium–high heat and add 1 tablespoon of the coconut oil. Add the lamb shanks and cook for 2 ½ minutes on each side, or until they are nicely browned. Remove from the heat and set aside.

Melt the remaining coconut oil in an ovenproof casserole dish over medium heat. Add the garlic and cook for 2 minutes, or until soft. Add the onion, rosemary, chilli and a small pinch of salt. Stir well and cook for a few minutes, or until the onion is soft. Add the carrot and celery, stir well and cook for a further 2 minutes. Stir in the tomato paste and cook for 2 minutes. Add the tomatoes and stir well. Remove from the heat.

Place the lamb and cauliflower in the casserole dish and pour over the stock. Cover first with a sheet of baking paper, then with a tight-fitting lid. Cook in the oven for 2 hours, or until the meat is just starting to come away from the bone. Add the cavolo nero and return to the oven to cook for another 5 minutes, or until the cavolo nero is just wilted.

Season with salt and pepper to taste and serve.

SERVES 4

Korean food is becoming more and more popular here in Australia, and rightly so – it is delicious. One of my favourite dishes is the super simple bibimbap, with all its wonderful ingredients that you place in a bowl and mix with raw or cooked egg, kimchi and some kick-ass chilli paste. It is usually served with rice but I love to eat it with cauliflower rice.

BEEF BIBIMBAP

SEASONED MUSHROOMS

1 teaspoon coconut oil

200 g shiitake mushrooms, sliced

2 tablespoons soy sauce

1 teaspoon sesame oil

SEASONED BEAN SPROUTS

1 teaspoon sea salt

200 g bean sprouts

2 spring onions, finely sliced

1 tablespoon sesame seeds, toasted

1 tablespoon sesame oil

SEASONED CARROTS

1 teaspoon coconut oil

2 carrots, cut into 5 cm batons

½ teaspoon sea salt

1 tablespoon sesame oil

SPICY CUCUMBER

½ telegraph cucumber, sliced

½ teaspoon sea salt

2 tablespoons Tangy Red Chilli Dressing (page 251), plus extra to serve

1 tablespoon sesame seeds, toasted

Ingredient list continued over page

To prepare the seasoned mushrooms, place a frying pan over medium heat. Add the coconut oil and mushrooms and cook for 2 minutes. Add the soy sauce and sesame oil, remove from the heat and transfer to a bowl.

For the seasoned bean sprouts, combine 125 ml of water with the salt and bean sprouts in a saucepan and bring to the boil. Reduce the heat to low, cover and steam for 5 minutes. Strain and transfer the sprouts to a bowl. Mix with the spring onions, toasted sesame seeds and sesame oil, then set aside.

For the seasoned carrots, melt the coconut oil in a frying pan over medium heat. Add the carrots and salt and stir-fry for 2 minutes, or until just tender. Drizzle with the sesame oil, transfer to a bowl and set aside.

For the spicy cucumber, toss the cucumber and salt in a large bowl and set aside for 5 minutes. Gently squeeze the cucumber with your hands to remove any excess liquid. Transfer to a new bowl, stir through the tangy red chilli dressing and sprinkle with the sesame seeds.

CONTINUED OVER PAGE ➤

BEEF BIBIMBAP (CONT.)

SEASONED SPINACH

1 bunch English spinach (about 450 g), trimmed

1 tablespoon sesame seeds, toasted

2 tablespoons dark sesame oil

1 teaspoon sea salt

SEASONED BEEF

500 g beef eye fillet or sirloin, cut into strips

1½ tablespoons soy sauce

1 teaspoon coconut oil

1 tablespoon honey

sea salt and freshly ground black pepper

½ teaspoon sesame oil

TO SERVE

2 cups Cauliflower Rice (page 248)

100 g wakame*

4 fried or hard-boiled eggs

150 g kimchi (for a recipe, see page 208)

See Glossary

For the seasoned spinach, fill a large saucepan with water and bring to the boil. Add the spinach and cook for 1 minute. Drain the spinach and rinse with cold water. Then, taking a handful of spinach at a time, gently squeeze out the water. Lay the spinach on a chopping board and cut into 5 cm pieces. Transfer to a bowl and add the sesame seeds, sesame oil and salt. Mix well.

For the seasoned beef, combine the beef, soy sauce, coconut oil and honey in a small bowl and mix well. Set aside to marinate for 15 minutes. Place a wok or large saucepan over medium–high heat, add the beef and stir-fry for 2 minutes. Season with salt and pepper to taste. Transfer to a bowl and top with the sesame oil.

To serve, arrange the cauliflower rice in the middle of a platter. Carefully arrange each of the seasoned salads, the wakame and the kimchi on top of the rice or in small bowls around it. Arrange the beef and an egg on each plate and drizzle with the extra tangy red chilli dressing.

SERVES 4

Beef cheeks were often on restaurant menus when I was a young chef, and when cooked correctly, they have the most amazing flavour. Beef cheeks come from the hard-working muscles on either side of the cheekbones. Any muscle that is constantly worked becomes very tough; therefore, when you cook cheeks, you need to do so on a low temperature for a very long time to allow the muscle fibres to break down and become melt-in-the-mouth tender. My money is always spent on secondary cuts like cheek, tail or leg meat for flavour, and I only use prize cuts like eye fillet for raw preparations or extra-special dishes.

BURMESE BEEF CHEEK CURRY

AUBERGINE PICKLE

1 aubergine

sea salt

2 teaspoons dried garlic

1 small onion, finely chopped

½ teaspoon chilli powder

1 teaspoon ground turmeric

½ teaspoon sea salt

1 teaspoon shrimp paste (belacan)*

3 tablespoons coconut oil

1 teaspoon apple cider vinegar*

½ teaspoon fish sauce*, or to taste

SPICE PASTE

8 dried red chillies

3 cm piece of fresh galangal*

3 cm piece of ginger

3 lemongrass stems, white part only, chopped

5 red Asian shallots

* See Glossary

Ingredient list continued over page

To make the aubergine pickle, cut the aubergine into 8 cm long batons. Place on a tray and sprinkle with some salt. Leave for 5–10 minutes, then rinse under cold water and pat dry.

Soak the dried garlic in 1 ½ teaspoons of hot water for 3 minutes, then mash to a paste. Mix with the onion, chilli powder, turmeric, salt and shrimp paste. Add the aubergine and stir well.

Heat the coconut oil in a frying pan over medium heat and fry the aubergine for about 5 minutes, turning over so that it cooks evenly. Reduce the heat to low, pour 3 tablespoons of water over the aubergine, cover and simmer for 5 minutes, or until the liquid is absorbed. Add the apple cider vinegar and fish sauce and continue to cook, moving the aubergine carefully in the pan, for 2 minutes, or until the oil becomes relatively clear. Remove from the heat and set aside.

To make the spice paste, soak the dried red chillies in warm water for 5–10 minutes, then drain. Place the chillies in a food processor with all the other ingredients and process to a paste.

CONTINUED OVER PAGE ➤

BURMESE BEEF CHEEK CURRY (CONT.)

3 teaspoons tamarind pulp*

2 tablespoons coconut oil

600 g beef cheeks

3 cardamom pods

3 whole cloves

3 star anise

1 cinnamon stick

1 lemongrass stem, white part only

6 kaffir lime leaves*

30 g shredded coconut, toasted

400 ml coconut cream

½ bunch of kale (about 200 g)

200 g choy sum

2 tablespoons fried shallots (for a recipe, see page 252)

* See Glossary

Mix the tamarind pulp with 125 ml of warm water in a bowl and, using your fingers, extract the juice from the tamarind pulp. Strain, discarding the pulp and seeds and reserving the tamarind water.

Heat the coconut oil in a large saucepan over medium heat. Add the spice paste and fry for 2–3 minutes, or until fragrant. Add the beef cheeks and seal them in the spice mix on all sides. Add the tamarind water, spices, lemongrass, kaffir lime leaves, coconut, coconut cream and 300 ml of water, cover and simmer over low heat for 2 hours, or until the cheeks are tender. Add the kale and choy sum and simmer for a further 2 minutes, or until wilted.

Serve the curry scattered with fried shallots and with the aubergine pickle on the side.

SERVES 4

TIPS

This dish is inspired by a Burmese curry but please feel free to look to other cuisines for inspiration. And if cheeks aren't your thing, then use another secondary cut like tail, gravy beef or shin.

Activated nuts are quite trendy in the health industry and they're becoming more and more popular. Activated basically means that the nuts have been soaked, so that they sprout, which releases their enzyme inhibitors. Enzyme inhibitors, such as phytic and oxalic acid, prevent nuts from sprouting at inappropriate times, but they also make them difficult to digest. Once soaked, you can eat them raw, blend them into silky nut milks, dehydrate them in a dehydrator, or bake them on a very low heat in your oven to regain their dry, crunchy texture. During this process you can add spices and herbs to make them really flavoursome.

ACTIVATED NUTS

400 g whole nuts (try almonds, brazil nuts, macadamia nuts, hazelnuts, pecans, walnuts, pistachio nuts or cashews)

sea salt, garlic salt, onion powder, tamari* or curry powder (optional)

* See Glossary

Place the nuts in a bowl, add enough filtered water to cover, then set aside to soak. The length of time you need to soak for will depend on the type of nut you use. The harder the nut, the longer the soaking time. Soak almonds for at least 12 hours; brazil nuts and macadamia nuts for 8 hours; pecans, walnuts and pistachio nuts for 4–6 hours; and cashews for 2–4 hours.

After soaking, the nuts will look nice and puffy, and may even start to show signs of sprouting.

Rinse the nuts under running water and pat dry. If you want to add flavour, now is the time to do it. Just shake a couple of teaspoons of whichever seasoning you like over the nuts and stir well.

To toast the nuts without damaging all those nutrients we've activated, dry them out using low heat – either in a dehydrator or on the lowest temperature in your oven, which is usually 50°C. This will take anywhere from 6–24 hours, depending on the temperature you're using. The nuts are done when they feel and taste dry.

Use the activated nuts as you would normally use toasted nuts. They can also be ground and used for baking. Store in an airtight container in the pantry for up to 3 months.

MAKES 400 G

These seed crackers are a fabulous alternative to store-bought varieties, and kids love them.

BASIL AND PARSLEY PESTO

I have been making pesto for decades now. This version is dairy-free and uses parsley as well as basil. It is perfect served with seed crackers (see recipe below) as a pre-dinner snack.

2 very large handfuls of basil leaves

2 very large handfuls of flat-leaf parsley leaves

2 garlic cloves, roughly chopped

1 tablespoon pine nuts, toasted

2 tablespoons lemon juice

12 macadamia nuts (activated if possible, see page 176)

80 ml macadamia oil or extra-virgin olive oil

sea salt and freshly ground black pepper

Place all the ingredients in food processor and combine to form a thick paste. Taste and adjust seasoning. The pesto will keep for up to 5 days in the fridge.

MAKES ABOUT 400 ML

TIP

Fresh basil and basil oil have been shown to stop the growth of many bacteria, even some that have become resistant to antibiotics. Basil oil is also a great source of magnesium, which helps the body's blood vessels relax and can improve blood flow. So toss a few basil leaves into your favourite dish for a fresh burst of flavour and reap the health benefits at the same time.

SEED CRACKERS

There are so many choices in the biscuit aisle at the supermarket, but have you ever read the ingredients on the packets? I find it astonishing that manufacturers are allowed to create these 'non-foods'. So what are your options? You can go to a health food store and pay an exorbitant amount for some crackers, or you can make your own for a fraction of the cost. You will need to start this recipe the day before.

160 g golden or brown linseeds

80 g mixed seeds, such as pumpkin, sunflower, sesame

½ teaspoon sea salt

1 teaspoon of your favourite spice, such as cayenne pepper, smoked paprika, cumin seeds or fennel seeds

Place the linseeds in a bowl and cover with water. Place the other seeds in a separate bowl and cover with water. Leave the seeds to soak overnight.

The next morning, drain and rinse the mixed seeds and add them to the undrained, jelly-like linseeds. Add the salt and spice and stir well.

Preheat the oven to 50°C, or as low as it will go. Spread the mixture very thinly on a couple of baking trays and bake for about 6 hours, turning over halfway through to help the drying process. Remove from the oven and cool on the trays.

Break into pieces and serve with your favourite dips or pâté. The crackers can be stored in an airtight container for up to 2 weeks.

SERVES 4

Kale chips are big in the health world due to kale's high levels of iron, vitamin K, vitamin C, calcium and antioxidants. It's no wonder people refer to kale as a 'nutritional powerhouse'. Potatoes have always been the predominant ingredient for chips, but potatoes are, in fact, anti-nutrient vegetables because they contain enzyme blockers, lectins and another family of toxins called glycoalkaloids, which aren't destroyed by cooking. I haven't eaten spuds for a long time and I find that sweet potato, pumpkin and kale more than make up for them.

KALE CHIPS

1 bunch of kale (about 400 g)

1 tablespoon coconut oil, melted

sea salt or Himalayan salt

Preheat the oven to 120°C. Line 2 trays with baking paper.

Wash the kale thoroughly with cold water and pat dry. Remove and discard the tough central stalk from the kale leaves, then cut or tear into smaller pieces.

In a large bowl, toss the kale with the coconut oil and some salt – go easy on the salt as a little goes a long way. Place the kale on the tray in a single layer. (Make sure you don't overcrowd – use an extra tray if you need to.) Roast for 35–40 minutes, or until crispy. Eat immediately or store in an airtight container in the pantry for up to 2 weeks.

SERVES 2

VARIATION

Try adding different flavourings to the kale, such as chilli powder, smoked paprika, cumin or sesame seeds.

TIP

You can use a dehydrator instead of an oven for this recipe. Just do a little research before purchasing one as they are generally made of plastic and the jury is still out on the effects that a plastic dehydrator may have on food.

Maca powder is made from the root of the maca plant, which is native to the Andean mountains of Peru and Bolivia. It is full of vitamins, minerals and all of the essential amino acids, and is also believed to be an aphrodisiac. These delicious balls are a great way to add some maca, as well as chia seeds, into your diet.

DATE, CHIA AND MACA BALLS

15 pitted dates, chopped

50 g chia seeds*

1 teaspoon maca powder*

1 teaspoon ground cinnamon

50 g slivered almonds

75 g walnuts (activated if possible, see page 176), crushed

3–4 tablespoons shredded coconut

* See Glossary

Combine the dates, chia seeds, maca powder, cinnamon, almonds, walnuts and 3 tablespoons of the coconut in a bowl and mix well.

Place the remaining 2 tablespoons of coconut in another bowl. Take small amounts of the mixture and roll into balls. Coat the balls in the coconut, rolling them around in your palms so that the coconut sticks. Store in the fridge for up to 2 weeks.

MAKES 12

VARIATION

You can use any type of nut in this recipe. You can also add another type of dried fruit, such as figs or apricots.

Cashew turmeric spread
(see recipe on page 187)

Beetroot hummus
(see recipe on page 186)

Muhammara

Muhammara is a Syrian red pepper dip that is also found in Palestinian and Lebanese cuisine. It has a wonderful flavour that is sweet, sharp, hot and moreish. Superb when teamed with protein such as eggs, fish, chicken or steak, it is also delicious served as a dip with raw vegetables or seed crackers (page 179).

MUHAMMARA

2–3 large red peppers, weighing about 500 g

50 g walnuts (activated if possible, see page 176)

50 g macadamia nuts (activated if possible, see page 176)

1 teaspoon cumin seeds

½ teaspoon sea salt

¼ teaspoon smoked paprika

pinch of chilli powder or cayenne pepper

1 garlic clove, peeled

2 teaspoons macadamia oil or extra-virgin olive oil

2 teaspoons lemon juice

1 tablespoon pomegranate molasses*

* See Glossary

Preheat the oven to 220°C.

Place the peppers on a tray and bake, turning occasionally, for 15 minutes, or until they start to blister and blacken. Remove from the oven, place in a large bowl and cover tightly with foil. Allow the peppers to soften for 10–20 minutes then remove the foil and peel the skin off. Pull off the stems, open the peppers and use a teaspoon to gently scoop away the remaining seeds and membranes. Set aside.

Toast the walnuts, macadamia nuts and cumin seeds in a dry frying pan over medium heat for 2–5 minutes, or until fragrant.

Transfer the nuts and seeds to a food processor. Add the peppers, salt, paprika, chilli powder or cayenne pepper, garlic, oil, lemon juice and pomegranate molasses and process to a smooth paste. The muhammara will keep in the fridge for up to 5 days.

MAKES ABOUT 450 G

If you are following a paleo diet, then you are probably steering clear of all legumes and pulses. One of the hardest things I found about giving up legumes was missing out on hummus. But then I stumbled across this great alternative, which not only tastes delicious but has the added bonus of nutrient-dense beetroot. You can also try this with carrot for another wonderful spread.

BEETROOT HUMMUS

500 g beetroot

3 tablespoons unhulled tahini*

1 garlic clove

2 tablespoons extra-virgin olive oil

2 tablespoons lemon juice

1 tablespoon apple cider vinegar*

2 teaspoons ground cumin

½ teaspoon sea salt

TO SERVE
Seed Crackers (page 179)

raw vegetables, such as carrot, broccoli, celery and cucumber, cut into bite-sized pieces

* See Glossary

Preheat the oven to 200°C.

Wrap the beetroot in foil and roast in the oven for 30–40 minutes, or until tender. Set aside to cool. When cool enough to handle, peel and roughly chop.

Place the beetroot in a food processor with all the other ingredients. Process until smooth. Transfer to a bowl, adjust the seasoning and serve with seed crackers and raw vegetables. The hummus can be stored in the fridge for up to 5 days.

MAKES ABOUT 500 ML

Peanut butter is a staple in many homes and kids are brought up to slather it on bread or toast. I never enjoyed the flavour or texture of peanut butter, and I definitely didn't enjoy how I felt after eating it. It wasn't until years later that I discovered peanuts are actually legumes and the human body finds them extremely difficult to digest. In saying that, I do believe nut and seed spreads can be delicious and nutritious if you make them yourself with some great ingredients. My good mate Pete Melov has been making nut spreads for years and he has kindly shared this recipe with us. You will need to start this recipe the day before.

CASHEW TURMERIC SPREAD

160 g brazil nuts

600 g cashews (you can also use almonds or macadamia nuts)

1 tablespoon ground turmeric

500 ml coconut oil, melted

½ teaspoon sea salt

1 tablespoon pau d'arco powder*

1 tablespoon slippery elm powder*

1 tablespoon raw protein meal (optional)

TO SERVE

Pete's Sprouted Seed Bread (page 23)

raw vegetables, such as carrot, pepper and cauliflower, cut into bite-sized pieces

* See Glossary

Place the brazil nuts in a bowl, cover with water and soak for 8 hours or overnight. Place the cashews in a separate bowl, cover with water and soak for 4 hours.

Drain the nuts. Place all the ingredients in a food processor and pulse to mix. Continue pulsing until you reach the consistency you like, adding more melted coconut oil if you prefer a runnier spread. Transfer to a bowl and serve with toasted sprouted seed bread and raw vegetables. Store in the fridge for up to 2 weeks.

MAKES ABOUT 1.2 KG

TIP

Raw protein meal is available at health food stores, but if you can't find any this spread will still be delicious and incredibly good for you.

I'm a sucker for olives. I love eating them at any time of the day, especially when I'm cooking, but when I was a kid I couldn't stand them. The thing that turned me off was trying them on a pizza. You may remember the poor excuses for olives that they put on pizzas – they didn't even taste real! It wasn't until I began cooking professionally that I realised there were actually many different kinds of olive, each with their own flavours and characteristics. Olives have anti-inflammatory and antioxidant properties, as well as dozens of valuable nutrients, which makes them an ideal snack or side.

ROASTED OLIVES

1 teaspoon fennel seeds

1 teaspoon cumin seeds

1 teaspoon coriander seeds

120 g mixed olives, with or without pits

zest of 1 orange or lemon, sliced into 1 cm strips

¼ teaspoon sea salt

¼ teaspoon freshly ground black pepper

1 tablespoon coconut oil

1 tablespoon sherry vinegar

1 garlic clove, finely chopped

pinch of dried chilli flakes

1–2 rosemary sprigs, leaves picked

2 thyme sprigs

Preheat the oven to 175°C.

Combine the fennel, cumin and coriander seeds in a dry frying pan and toast over medium heat, shaking the pan often to evenly distribute the spices, for about 5 minutes, or until fragrant.

Combine the olives, orange or lemon peel, salt, pepper, oil, vinegar, garlic, chilli flakes and herbs in a bowl. Add the toasted seeds and mix well.

Arrange the olives on a baking tray and roast for 15 minutes. Serve hot with napkins, a little bowl for the pits and two glasses of wine.

SERVES 2

DUKKAH

Dukkah is an Egyptian side dish consisting of herbs, nuts, seeds and spices. I love to sprinkle it over grilled fish or meat or salads, add it to soups and tagines or serve it with sprouted seed bread (page 23), cashew cheese (below) and some extra-virgin olive oil. One thing is for sure; once you make it, it won't last long!

80 g pine nuts

40 g coriander seeds

120 g sesame seeds

½ teaspoon ground cumin

½ teaspoon sea salt

½ teaspoon chilli powder

½ teaspoon baharat*

pinch of dried mint

* *See Glossary*

Combine the pine nuts and coriander seeds in a large, dry frying pan and toast over medium–high heat for 1 minute, or until the mix has started to colour. Add the sesame seeds and toast for another minute, or until golden brown.

Pour the nut and seed mix into a food processor. Add the cumin, salt, chilli powder, baharat and mint and pulse to combine.

Store the dukkah in an airtight container in the pantry for 2–3 weeks.

MAKES ABOUT 250 G

CASHEW CHEESE

This is one of my all-time favourite treats. We serve it with raw vegetables, seed crackers (page 179) or sprouted seed bread (page 23). It's also great for adding another textural dimension to salads, such as the spicy beetroot, leek and walnut salad (page 80).

160 g cashews

2 teaspoons lemon juice

½ teaspoon sea salt

pinch of freshly ground black pepper

Soak the cashews in 750 ml of water for 4 hours. Drain and rinse well.

Place the cashews in a food processor. Add the lemon juice, salt and pepper and pulse for a minute to combine. Add 3 tablespoons of water and continue to process until smooth.

The cashew cheese can be stored in the fridge for up to 7 days.

MAKES ABOUT 200 G

VARIATIONS

You can use macadamia nuts instead of cashews, or perhaps add some flavoured oil, like truffle (see Glossary) or chilli oil.

Serve your cashew cheese and dukkah on a slice
of toasted sprouted seed bread (page 23).

Nic makes these spirulina balls from time to time and they are a favourite of mine. Spirulina is a blue-green algae that is harvested for its nutritional properties. It is full of protein and has a unique flavour that is quite strong at first. If you're anything like me, once you get used to it, you will look forward to eating it as you know it's doing your body so much good. Use any kind of nuts in this recipe – almonds, brazil nuts, cashews, walnuts or a mixture.

COCONUT AND SPIRULINA BALLS

1 cup chopped nuts of your choice (activated if possible, see page 176)

2 tablespoons coconut flour

1 teaspoon honey

½ teaspoon cinnamon

40 g coconut flakes

3 tablespoons chia seeds*

1 tablespoon spirulina*

100 ml unhulled tahini*

3 tablespoons coconut oil, melted

extra chia seeds*, for rolling

shredded coconut, for rolling

* See Glossary

Place the nuts, coconut flour, honey, cinnamon, coconut flakes, chia seeds, spirulina and tahini in a blender or food processor and process until smooth. While the motor is running, slowly add the melted coconut oil and process until well combined.

Place the extra chia seeds and shredded coconut in separate bowls. Wet your hands a little and roll the mixture into small balls, then roll them in the chia seeds and shredded coconut. Refrigerate for at least 20 minutes, or until firm. Enjoy!

MAKES ABOUT 14 BALLS

These jellies are a great way to treat your kids without giving them lots of refined sugar. Flavoured with natural fruit juice and sweetened with honey, they are perfect for filling lolly bags at a party or for special occasions.

FRUIT JUICE JELLIES

80 ml freshly squeezed juice, strained (try using lemons, apples, pears, blueberries, beetroots or oranges)

1–3 tablespoons honey, according to taste

1½ tablespoons good-quality powdered gelatine*

* See Glossary

Place the juice and honey in a saucepan and sprinkle over the powdered gelatine. Stir until the gelatine is incorporated, then allow to stand for 5 minutes.

Cook over medium heat, stirring constantly, for about 5 minutes, or until completely smooth. Make sure you don't boil the mixture. Pour into an ice-cube tray or chocolate moulds immediately and place in the freezer for about 15 minutes, or until set.

Once the jellies have set, remove from the tray and store in an airtight jar. They will be fine for a few weeks at room temperature – that's if your kids don't eat them all!

SERVES 2 VERY LUCKY KIDS

VARIATIONS

For yellow jellies, use lemon juice and add ¼–½ teaspoon of ground turmeric before cooking.

If you want purple jellies, place ⅓ cup of frozen blueberries in a saucepan and just cover with water. Simmer over low heat for about 5 minutes, or until the water is bright purple. Strain the liquid and add enough lemon juice or water to bring it up to 80 ml. Return the liquid to the clean saucepan, add the honey and gelatine and proceed with the method above.

TIPS

Use ice-cube trays with different shapes to make these treats more fun. And for ease of cleaning, make sure you wash the saucepan and cooking utensils immediately in hot, soapy water.

Fermented or cultured food is the newest craze, which is funny as it is actually one of the oldest ways of preserving food. If you are interested in learning more about fermentation, try reading *Wild Fermentation* by Sandor Katz, a good mate of mine. Sandor explains the history of fermentation so eloquently that you will be jumping into the kitchen to start your own cultured concoctions. Think of fermented foods as nature's probiotics, full of healthy lactic acid bacteria. Eating a small amount of fermented veg, like this delicious sauerkraut, with every meal will help to balance your gut flora.

SAUERKRAUT

1 star anise

1 teaspoon whole cloves

½ cabbage (about 600 g)
(you can use green or red, or a mix of the two)

1 ½ teaspoons sea salt

2 teaspoons caraway seeds

2 tablespoons juniper berries*

1 sachet vegetable starter culture*
 (this will weigh 2–5 g, depending on the brand)

* *See Glossary*

You will need a 1.5-litre preserving jar with an airlock lid for this recipe. Wash the jar and utensils thoroughly in very hot water or run them through a hot rinse cycle in the dishwasher.

Place the star anise and cloves in a small piece of muslin, tie into a bundle and set aside.

Remove the outer leaves of the cabbage. Choose one of the outer leaves, wash it well and set aside. Shred the cabbage in a food processor, or slice by hand or with a mandolin, then place in a large glass or stainless steel bowl. Sprinkle the salt, caraway seeds and juniper berries over the cabbage. Mix well, cover and set aside while you prepare the starter culture.

Dissolve the starter culture in water according to the packet instructions (the amount of water will depend on the brand you are using). Add to the cabbage with the muslin bag containing the spices and mix well.

Fill the prepared jar with the cabbage mix, pressing down well with a large spoon or potato masher to remove any air pockets. Leave 2 cm of room free at the top. The cabbage should be completely submerged in the liquid, so add more water if necessary.

Take the clean cabbage leaf, fold it up and place it on top of the mixture, then add a small glass weight to keep everything submerged (a small shot glass is ideal). Close the lid, then wrap a tea towel around the side of the jar to block out the light. Store in a dark place with a temperature of 16–23°C for 10–14 days. (You can place the jar in an esky to maintain a more consistent temperature.) Different vegetables have different culturing times and the warmer it is the shorter the time needed. The longer you leave the jar, the higher the level of good bacteria present. It is up to you how long you leave it – some people prefer the tangier flavour that comes with extra fermenting time, while others prefer a milder flavour.

Chill before eating. Once opened, it will last for up to 2 months in the fridge when kept submerged in the liquid. If unopened, it will keep for up to 9 months in the fridge.

MAKES 1 × 1.5-LITRE JAR

TIP

I use a Culture For Life starter jar as they are purpose-made for fermenting vegetables. If you do use one of these, there is no need to cover and weight the shredded cabbage with a folded cabbage leaf and shot glass, as the jar has an in-built weighting system. There is also no need to cover with a tea towel, as there is a silicone cover provided to block out the light.

Whenever I am preparing meals that are light and fresh I tend to opt for this beautiful summer kraut as a side dish. My good mate Kitsa created this recipe for me and it works really well with seafood, salads, stir-fries, curries and anything from South-East Asia, such as Vietnamese chicken salad (page 141). It is great to experiment with your own flavour combinations, so don't hold back.

SUMMER KRAUT WITH PINEAPPLE AND MINT

½ small cabbage (about 500 g)

1 large handful of kale (about 50 g), central stalk removed

½ small fennel bulb (about 100 g), trimmed

1 small red onion

2 red apples, cored but not peeled

1 small handful of mint leaves

¼ small pineapple (about 200 g), chopped

1½ teaspoons sea salt

1 sachet vegetable starter culture* (this will weigh 2–5 g, depending on the brand)

See Glossary

You will need a 1.5-litre preserving jar with an airlock lid for this recipe. Wash the jar and utensils thoroughly in very hot water or run them through a hot rinse cycle in the dishwasher.

Remove the outer leaves of the cabbage, choose one, wash it well and set aside for later.

Put a few pieces of cabbage in a food processor, followed by some kale, fennel, onion, apple and mint, so that the ingredients are mixed thoroughly. Remove from the processor and continue with the next batch until all the ingredients are shredded. (You can also use a mandolin or knife to chop, then mix by hand.) Transfer to a large glass or stainless steel bowl. Stir through the pineapple, sprinkle over the salt, cover and set aside.

Dissolve the starter culture in water according to the packet instructions (the amount of water will depend on the brand you are using). Add to the bowl of vegetables and mix again. Fill the prepared jar with the cabbage mix, pressing down well with a large spoon or potato masher to remove any air pockets. Leave 2 cm of room free at the top. The cabbage mix should be completely submerged in the liquid, so add more water if necessary.

Take the clean cabbage leaf, fold it up and place it on top of the mixture, then add a small glass weight to keep everything submerged (a small shot glass is ideal). Close the lid, then wrap a tea towel around the side of the jar to block out the light. Store in a dark place with a temperature of 16–23°C for 10–14 days. (You can place the jar in an esky to maintain a more consistent temperature.) Different vegetables have different culturing times and the warmer it is the shorter the time needed. The longer you leave the jar, the higher the level of good bacteria present. It's up to you how long you leave it – some people prefer the tangier flavour that comes with extra fermenting time, while others prefer a milder flavour.

Chill before eating. Once opened, it will last for up to 2 months in the fridge when kept submerged in the liquid. If unopened, it will keep for up to 9 months in the fridge.

MAKES 1 × 1.5-LITRE JAR

TIP

I use a Culture For Life starter jar as they are purpose-made for fermenting vegetables. If you do use one of these, there is no need to cover and weight the shredded cabbage with a folded cabbage leaf and shot glass, as the jar has an in-built weighting system. There is also no need to cover with a tea towel as there is a silicone cover provided to block out the light.

One of my aims with this book is to help you eliminate the bad stuff from your pantry and fridge – those ingredients and products that have no nutritional value and are doing harm to your body. This doesn't mean you have to go without, it is just a matter of replacing the bad with the good. So here is a recipe for tomato ketchup that doesn't contain any of the nasty stuff. Kids and adults alike will love it on their sausages, steaks and eggs. I've adapted this recipe from Sally Fallon's *Nourishing Traditions*, which is one of my favourite cookbooks.

CULTURED TOMATO KETCHUP

500 g good-quality or homemade tomato paste

3 tablespoons honey or maple syrup

⅓ sachet vegetable starter culture*

2 tablespoons lemon juice, plus extra to thin

1 teaspoon sea salt

freshly ground black pepper

1 garlic clove, finely chopped

1 long red chilli, halved, seeded and finely sliced

1 teaspoon ground allspice

½ teaspoon ground cloves

* *See Glossary*

You will need a 750 ml preserving jar with an airlock lid for this recipe. Wash the jar and utensils thoroughly in very hot water or run them through a hot rinse cycle in the dishwasher.

Place the tomato paste in a large bowl and fold through the honey or maple syrup. Whisk in the vegetable starter culture along with 120 ml of water, the lemon juice, salt, a few grinds of black pepper, garlic, chilli, allspice and cloves. Continue whisking until smooth. Add some extra lemon juice if you'd like a thinner sauce. Spoon into the preserving jar and close the lid. Wrap a tea towel around the side of the jar to block out the light.

Store in a dark place with a temperature of 16–23°C for 3–5 days. (You can place the jar in an esky to maintain a more consistent temperature.) The warmer the weather the shorter the amount of time needed. The longer you leave the jar, the higher the level of good bacteria present. It is up to you how long you leave it to ferment – some people prefer the tangier flavour that results from a longer fermenting time, while others prefer a milder flavour. Give the ketchup a good stir before transferring to the refrigerator, where it will keep for several months.

MAKES 1 × 750 ML JAR

Mustard is a wonderful addition to so many recipes and meals, whether it's used to add oomph to mayo or to a simple dressing of apple cider vinegar, herbs and extra-virgin olive oil, or simply served with your steak or burger. It adds a lovely texture and mouth-puckering flavour.

FERMENTED MUSTARD

185 ml fermented brine liquid, strained from one of the sauerkrauts (pages 198–201)

80 g brown and yellow mustard seeds (brown are hotter and will make a spicier mustard)

1 French shallot, finely chopped

2 garlic cloves, finely chopped

1 tablespoon maple syrup

sea salt

You will need a 250 ml preserving jar with an airlock lid for this recipe. Wash the jar and utensils thoroughly in very hot water or run them through a hot rinse cycle in the dishwasher. Drain on a clean tea towel.

Combine the fermented brine liquid, mustard seeds, shallot and garlic in a glass or stainless steel bowl, cover with a plate and allow to soak at room temperature overnight.

In a food processor, combine the soaked seed mixture with the maple syrup and process. If you like lots of whole seeds in your mustard, you will only need to process for a minute or two; if you like a smooth mustard, process for longer until you have a texture you are happy with. Check the seasoning and add sea salt to taste.

Store in the preserving jar in the fridge, where it will keep for up to 3 months.

MAKES 1 × 250 ML JAR

My dear friend Kitsa Yanniotis has an amazing business called Kitsa's Kitchen, which supplies delicious fermented vegetables to health food stores around the country. Kitsa has been kind enough to share this delicious winter kraut recipe and I am sure you are going to love it.

WINTER KRAUT WITH BEETROOT AND GOJI BERRIES

50 g goji berries*

100 ml coconut water* (if using packaged, ensure it has no additives)

1 star anise

1 teaspoon whole cloves

½ small red cabbage (about 600 g)

2 beetroot (about 300 g in total)

2 Granny Smith apples, cored but not peeled

1½ teaspoons sea salt

1 sachet vegetable starter culture* (this will weigh 2–5 g, depending on the brand)

See Glossary

You will need a 1.5-litre preserving jar with an airlock lid for this recipe. Wash the jar and utensils thoroughly in very hot water or run them through a hot rinse cycle in the dishwasher.

Place the goji berries in a small bowl with the coconut water and set aside to rehydrate for a couple of hours.

Wrap the star anise and cloves in a small piece of muslin, tie into a bundle and set aside.

Remove the outer leaves of the cabbage. Choose one, wash it well, then set aside for later. Put a few pieces of cabbage in a food processor, followed by some beetroot, then some apple, so that all the ingredients are mixed thoroughly. Remove from the processor and continue with the next batch until all the ingredients are shredded. (You can also use a mandolin or knife to chop, then mix by hand.) Transfer to a large glass

Cultured kale with fennel
and beetroot leaves
(see recipe on page 206)

Cultured beetroot.
apple and carrot (see
recipe on page 207)

Winter kraut with beetroot
and goji berries

or stainless steel bowl and add the salt, rehydrated goji berries and coconut water. Mix well, then cover with a plate and set aside.

Dissolve the starter culture in water according to the packet instructions (the amount of water will depend on the brand). Add to the bowl of vegetables along with the muslin bag containing the spices and mix again. Fill the prepared jar with the cabbage mix, pressing down well with a large spoon or potato masher to remove any air pockets. Leave 2 cm of room free at the top. The cabbage mix should be completely submerged in the liquid. If you don't have enough liquid, add more water until you do.

Take the clean outer cabbage leaf, fold it up and place it on top of the mixture, then add a small glass weight to keep everything submerged (a small shot glass is ideal). Close the lid to seal, then wrap a tea towel around the side of the jar to block out the light, leaving the airlock exposed.

Store in a dark place with a temperature of 16–23°C for 10–14 days. (You can place the jar in an esky to maintain a more consistent temperature.) Different vegetables have different culturing times and the warmer the weather the shorter the amount of time needed. The longer you leave the jar, the higher the level of good bacteria present. It's up to you how long you leave it to ferment – some people prefer the tangier flavour that results from a longer fermenting time, while others prefer a milder flavour.

Chill before eating. Once opened, it will last for up to 2 months in the fridge when kept submerged in the liquid. If unopened, it will keep for up to 9 months in the fridge.

MAKES 1 × 1.5-LITRE JAR

As a chef, I am always playing around with recipes and ingredients. I recently made an amazing salad using kale, fennel and beetroot leaves, and it occurred to me that these three ingredients would also make a really nice cultured veg preparation. Experiment with whatever vegetables are in season and see what you come up with.

CULTURED KALE WITH FENNEL AND BEETROOT LEAVES

1 teaspoon whole cloves

½ bunch of kale (about 250 g), central stalk removed

200 g beetroot leaves, washed well and cut into 1 cm thick slices

1 small fennel bulb (about 200 g), finely shredded

2 teaspoons sea salt or Himalayan salt

2 teaspoons fennel seeds

2 teaspoons juniper berries*

1 sachet vegetable starter culture* (this will weigh 2–5 g, depending on the brand)

* See Glossary

You will need a 1-litre preserving jar with an airlock lid for this recipe. Wash the jar and utensils thoroughly in very hot water or run them through a hot rinse cycle in the dishwasher.

Place the cloves in a small piece of muslin, tie into a bundle and set aside.

Choose a kale leaf, wash it well and set aside. Wash, pat dry and shred the remaining kale. Combine the kale, beetroot leaves and fennel in a large glass or stainless steel bowl. Sprinkle on the salt and mix, then add the fennel seeds and juniper berries and mix again. Cover with a plate and set aside.

Dissolve the starter culture in water according to the packet instructions (the amount of water will depend on the brand). Add to the bowl of vegetables along with the muslin bag containing the cloves and mix again. Fill the prepared jar with the vegetable mix, pressing down well with a large spoon or potato masher to remove any air pockets. Leave 2 cm of room free at the top. The vegetables should be completely submerged in the liquid, so add more water if necessary.

Fold the clean kale leaf, place it on top of the mixture and add a small glass weight to keep everything submerged (a small shot glass is ideal). Close the lid, then wrap a tea towel around the side of the jar to block out the light. Store in a dark place with a temperature of 16–23°C for 10–14 days. (You can place the jar in an esky to maintain a more consistent temperature.) Different vegetables have different culturing times and the warmer it is the shorter the time needed. The longer you leave the jar, the higher the level of good bacteria present and the tangier the flavour.

Chill before eating. Once opened, it will last for up to 2 months in the fridge when kept submerged in the liquid. If unopened, it will keep for up to 9 months in the fridge.

MAKES 1 × 1-LITRE JAR

This is one of my favourite cultured recipes. It works so well with fish, eggs, chicken, game meat, beef and pork – actually, any kind of protein. Try this in a burger instead of a slice of canned beetroot and you will be transported to another place altogether. Make this recipe when beetroot is in season.

CULTURED BEETROOT, APPLE AND CARROT

2 star anise

1 tablespoon whole cloves

3 large carrots

3 large beetroot, peeled

3 large apples, cored but not peeled (any kind of apple is fine)

1 tablespoon sea salt

1 sachet vegetable starter culture*
(this will weigh 2–5 g, depending on the brand)

1 large cabbage leaf, washed well and folded

* See Glossary

You will need a 1.5-litre preserving jar with an airlock lid for this recipe. Wash the jar and utensils thoroughly in very hot water or run them through a hot rinse cycle in the dishwasher.

Wrap the star anise and cloves in a small piece of muslin, tie and set aside.

Put a few pieces of carrot in a food processor, followed by some beetroot, then apple, so that the fruit and vegetables are mixed thoroughly. Remove from the processor and continue with the next batch until all the fruit and vegetables are shredded. (You can also use a mandolin or knife to chop, then mix by hand.) Transfer to a large glass or stainless steel bowl and add the muslin bag with spices. Sprinkle over the salt, mix well, then cover with a plate and set aside.

Dissolve the starter culture in water according to the packet instructions (the amount of water will depend on the brand). Add to the vegetable mix and combine. Fill the jar with the vegetable mix, pressing down well with a large spoon or potato masher to remove any air pockets. Leave 2 cm of room free at the top. The vegetable mix should be completely submerged in the liquid, so add more water if necessary.

Place the cabbage leaf on top of the mixture and add a small glass weight to keep everything submerged (a small shot glass is ideal). Close the lid, then wrap a tea towel around the jar to block out the light. Store in a dark place with a temperature of 16–23°C for 10–14 days. (You can place the jar in an esky to maintain a more consistent temperature.) Different vegetables have different culturing times and the warmer it is the shorter the time needed. The longer you leave the jar, the higher the level of good bacteria and the tangier the flavour.

Chill before eating. Once opened, it will last for up to 2 months in the fridge when kept submerged in the liquid. If unopened, it will keep for up to 9 months in the fridge.

MAKES 1 × 1.5-LITRE JAR

Kimchi is Korea's national dish and I love the fact that every Korean household makes it a little differently. It's basically fermented cabbage with spices, and I would avoid buying pre-prepared versions, as they can be heavily laden with sugar. Instead try this recipe – it's great with eggs, cauliflower rice (page 248) or any Asian dish, or try tossing it through a salad for extra bite.

KIMCHI WITH RADISH AND CORIANDER

½ Chinese cabbage (wong bok) (about 500 g)

3 radishes or 1 daikon*

1 carrot

1 onion

1½ teaspoons sea salt

3–4 garlic cloves, finely sliced

3 tablespoons grated ginger

3–4 long red chillies, halved, seeded and finely sliced

2 large handfuls of coriander roots, stems and leaves, finely chopped

1 tablespoon Korean chilli powder (gochugaru)* (optional)

1 teaspoon ground turmeric (optional)

1 sachet vegetable starter culture* (this will weigh 2–5 g, depending on the brand)

* See Glossary

You will need a 1.5-litre preserving jar with an airlock lid for this recipe. Wash the jar and utensils thoroughly in very hot water or run them through a hot rinse cycle in the dishwasher.

Remove the outer leaves of the cabbage. Choose one, wash it well and set aside. Finely shred the cabbage, radishes or daikon, carrots and onions in a food processor. (You can also use a mandolin or knife to chop them finely.) In a large glass or stainless steel bowl, combine the cabbage with the radish or daikon, carrot and onion. Sprinkle on the salt and mix well. Add the garlic, ginger, chillies, coriander, chilli powder and turmeric (if using). Mix well, cover and set aside.

Dissolve the starter culture in water according to the packet instructions (the amount of water will depend on the brand). Add to the vegetables and mix well. Fill the prepared jar with the vegetable mix, pressing down well with a large spoon or potato masher to remove any air pockets. Leave 2 cm of room free at the top. The vegetables should be completely submerged in the liquid, so add more water if necessary.

Fold the clean cabbage leaf, place it on top of the mixture and add a small glass weight to keep everything submerged (a small shot glass is ideal). Close the lid, then wrap a tea towel around the side of the jar to block out the light. Store in a dark place with a temperature of 16–23°C for 10–14 days. (You can place the jar in an esky to maintain a more consistent temperature.) Different vegetables have different culturing times and the warmer it is the shorter the time needed. The longer you leave the jar, the higher the level of good bacteria present and the tangier the flavour.

Chill before eating. Once opened, it will last for up to 2 months in the fridge when kept submerged in the liquid. If unopened, it will keep for up to 9 months in the fridge.

MAKES 1 × 1.5-LITRE JAR

Yes, I love chilli. I love it so much that my daughter is named Chilli. This fermented chilli sauce is a great staple to have on hand when you want to add some kick to your dishes without adding any sugar or preservatives. I use it to spice up eggs, stir-fries, curries or simple vegetable dishes.

FERMENTED HOT CHILLI SAUCE

1 sachet vegetable starter culture* (this will weigh 2–5 g, depending on the brand)

1.5 kg long red chillies

5 garlic cloves, peeled

2 tablespoons honey

2 teaspoons sea salt

* See Glossary.

You will need a 1.5-litre preserving jar with an airlock lid for this recipe. Wash the jar and utensils thoroughly in very hot water or run them through a hot rinse cycle in the dishwasher.

Dissolve the starter culture in water according to the packet instructions (the amount of water will depend on the brand).

Place the starter culture and all the remaining ingredients in a food processor and process to a fine paste. Spoon into the preserving jar, close the lid to seal, then wrap a tea towel around the side of the jar to block out the light, leaving the airlock exposed.

Store in a dark place with a temperature of 16–23°C for 5–7 days. (You can place the jar in an esky to maintain a more consistent temperature.)

After the chilli paste has bubbled and brewed for about a week, set a fine sieve over a bowl, tip the chilli paste into the sieve and press down with a wooden spoon to extract as much chilli sauce as possible.

Pour the sauce from the bowl into a clean 1-litre jar to store. Close the lid to seal and store in the refrigerator. The sauce will keep for several months in the fridge.

MAKES 1 × 1-LITRE JAR

If cheesecake is your thing but dairy isn't, then you'll love this recipe. You need a few tools for this one: a food processor and a drum sieve or good strainer. These cheesecakes are my girlfriend's one and only birthday request. Nic never wants presents or a foot rub, she just wants to go for our regular morning surf followed by a generous serving of raspberry mousse cheesecake. How can I argue with that?

RASPBERRY MOUSSE CHEESECAKES

450 g cashews

420 g raspberries (fresh or frozen)

100 ml lime juice

1 teaspoon sea salt

350 g honey

1 vanilla pod, split lengthways and seeds scraped

250 ml coconut oil

baby mint leaves (optional)

CRUMBLE

160 g almonds (activated if possible, see page 176)

90 g desiccated coconut

6 medjool dates, pitted

pinch of sea salt

½ teaspoon natural vanilla extract

CHOCOLATE SHAVINGS

120 ml coconut oil, melted

1½ tablespoons cacao powder*, sifted

1½ tablespoons carob powder*, sifted

1 tablespoon honey

* *See Glossary*

Soak the cashews for 4 hours, then rinse well.

To make the crumble, process the almonds and coconut in a food processor until broken up to a nice crumb. Add the dates, salt and vanilla extract and pulse until the mixture just comes together. If you over-process, the mixture will become oily. Transfer the crumble to a bowl and set aside.

Press the raspberries through a sieve. Set aside the leftover raspberry pulp.

Process the cashews, raspberry liquid, lime juice, salt, honey and vanilla seeds until the mixture is smooth and creamy. Add the coconut oil and process until combined. Pour the berry mixture into small glasses and refrigerate for a few hours, or until set.

To make the raspberry crunch, preheat the oven to 50°C, or as low as it will go. Spread the raspberry pulp on a lined baking tray and place it in the oven for a few hours. Remove from the oven and cool completely. You can chop the dried raspberry with a knife for a coarser texture, or blitz it in a food processor for a much finer consistency.

To make the chocolate shavings, mix the coconut oil, cacao powder, carob powder and honey in a bowl. Line a tray with baking paper and spread the mixture onto the paper as thinly as possible. Leave at room temperature for 5 minutes, then carefully roll the paper to form a cylinder and place it in the fridge for at least 10 minutes to harden. Once the chocolate has hardened, peel the paper away – you will be left with pretty chocolate shavings. Place these on a tray and put them back in the fridge for another 2–5 minutes to firm up again.

To serve, sprinkle the cheesecakes with crumble, then top with the chocolate shavings, raspberry crunch and mint leaves (if using). You can store any leftover raspberry crunch in an airtight container for up to 3 months.

SERVES 6–8

DESSERTS

This poached pear recipe is one of my favourite special-occasion desserts. The flavours are, quite simply, sublime – and refreshing, too. If you feel the need to impress your guests or treat your family, this one's a winner!

POACHED PEARS

1 litre coconut water *

4 thick slices of ginger

2 lemongrass stems, white part only, bruised

small pinch of saffron threads or a pinch of ground turmeric

4 large, very firm Beurre Bosc pears, peeled, halved and cored

3 tablespoons chopped almonds (activated if possible, see page 176) (optional)

* *See Glossary*

In a large saucepan, combine the coconut water, ginger, lemongrass and saffron or turmeric and bring to the boil. Gently lower the pear halves into the liquid, making sure they're fully submerged. Simmer, covered, for 45 minutes, or until the pears are just tender. Set aside to cool in the syrup.

Place the pears in serving bowls and scatter with almonds (if using).

SERVES 4

I love making sweet treats with vegetables. The best carrot cake I ever made was with carrots I gathered from my garden. If you use the freshest ingredients you can, you're guaranteed an incredible flavour. This cake is perfect served with a cup of chai ginger tea and shared with some loved ones.

CARROT CAKE

5 small carrots, grated and excess water squeezed out

185 ml maple syrup

10 medjool dates, pitted

coconut oil, for greasing

80 g coconut flour, sifted

1 tablespoon ground cinnamon

1 teaspoon ground ginger

½ teaspoon sea salt

1 teaspoon baking powder

80 g walnuts (activated if possible, see page 176), chopped

80 g macadamia nuts (activated if possible, see page 176), chopped

10 eggs

2 teaspoons natural vanilla extract

250 ml coconut oil, melted

COCONUT CITRUS ICING

90 g desiccated coconut

3 tablespoons coconut cream

2 tablespoons honey or maple syrup

zest of 2 lemons, grated (optional)

3 tablespoons coconut oil, melted

HONEY-GLAZED WALNUTS

3 tablespoons honey

80 g walnuts (activated if possible, see page 176)

Place the carrot in a bowl and pour over 60 ml of the maple syrup. Mix, cover and refrigerate for an hour.

Meanwhile, place the dates in a bowl and cover with warm water. Soak for at least 20 minutes, then drain and mash.

Preheat the oven to 180°C. Grease a 20 cm × 12 cm loaf tin with coconut oil and line with baking paper.

Combine the coconut flour, cinnamon, ginger, salt, baking powder, walnuts and macadamia nuts in a bowl.

In a separate large bowl, combine the eggs, vanilla, melted coconut oil, remaining maple syrup and date mixture. Add the dry ingredients and mix well. Add the carrot mixture and stir until well combined.

Pour the batter into the prepared tin and bake for about 50 minutes, or until a skewer inserted into the centre of the cake comes out clean. Turn the cake out onto a wire rack and allow to cool.

To make the icing, mix the coconut, coconut cream, honey or maple syrup and lemon zest (if using) in a bowl. Gradually add the melted coconut oil and mix until smooth.

To make the honey-glazed walnuts, heat the honey in a small saucepan for 1–2 minutes, or until it starts to bubble. Stir in the walnuts and cook for a further 30 seconds, stirring constantly. Remove from the heat and spread the walnuts on a tray to cool.

Once the cake has cooled, cover with the icing and decorate with the honey-glazed walnuts.

SERVES 8–10

I first met Luke Hines when he was a contestant on a TV series I was working on. We hit it off straight away. Not only is he a good bloke with a wicked sense of humour, he is also a paleo freak and a personal trainer to boot. He has put me through my paces in my home gym and has great attention to detail when it comes to doing things properly. Luke made this recipe at my house one evening and it was a big hit. He has kindly shared it with us here.

CHOCOCADO MOUSSE 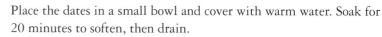 WITH RASPBERRIES

85 g medjool dates, pitted

2 ripe avocados, peeled and pitted

40 g cacao powder*

1 tablespoon honey or brown rice syrup*

1 teaspoon ground cinnamon

1 vanilla pod, split lengthways and seeds scraped

raspberries, to serve

toasted hazelnuts, to serve

* *See Glossary*

Place the dates in a small bowl and cover with warm water. Soak for 20 minutes to soften, then drain.

Place the dates, avocado, cacao, honey or brown rice syrup, cinnamon and vanilla seeds in a food processor and process until very smooth and fluffy.

Serve the mousse in small glasses topped with raspberries and hazelnuts.

SERVES 4

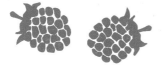

DESSERTS

This is the easiest coconut ice cream recipe in the world. You can jazz it up with extra ingredients if you wish, depending on what you intend to serve it with. If you prefer a creamier mixture, you can also add some coconut milk. And if you don't want to make popsicles, simply freeze this in a container and serve scoops of it in bowls.

YOUNG COCONUT POPSICLES

1 young coconut*

* See Glossary

Open the coconut by cutting a circular hole in the top. Pour the coconut water into a jug (you should get about 250 ml), then pour into ice-cube trays and freeze. Use a spoon to scoop the meat out of the coconut (you should get about 120 g). Place in the fridge until needed.

Once the ice cubes are fully frozen, place them in a high-speed blender or food processor with the coconut meat. Process until the mixture is completely smooth.

Pour into popsicle moulds and place in the freezer. After 1 hour, insert a popsicle stick into each one. Return to the freezer for at least 4 hours, or until frozen. You can enjoy your popsicles plain or try one of the flavour combinations below.

MAKES 4–6 POPSICLES

FLAVOUR VARIATIONS

Mango
Place 1 mango cheek in a blender or food processor and process until smooth. When filling the popsicle moulds with the coconut mixture, add 1 tablespoon of mango puree and swirl with the popsicle stick to mix.

Roasted strawberry
Roast 200 g strawberries in a 180°C oven for 10 minutes, or until tender. Allow to cool completely, then place in a blender or food processor and process until smooth. When filling the popsicle moulds with the coconut mixture, add 1 tablespoon of strawberry puree and swirl with the popsicle stick to mix.

This surprisingly easy but very satisfying recipe is the perfect after-work treat on a hot day. If you don't want to make popsicles, just freeze the mix in a plastic container and enjoy as ice cream.

BANANA POPSICLES

250 ml coconut water*

250 ml coconut cream or coconut milk

2 eggs

2 bananas, peeled, chopped and frozen

1 tablespoon honey

* See Glossary

Mix the coconut water and coconut cream or milk in a jug. Pour into ice-cube trays and place in the freezer for 4–5 hours, or until frozen.

Remove the trays from the freezer and place the coconut ice cubes in a blender or food processor with the eggs, bananas and honey. Process until smooth.

Pour the mix into popsicle moulds, freeze for 1 hour, then insert a popsicle stick into each one. Return to the freezer for at least 4 hours, or until frozen. You can enjoy your banana popsicles plain or try one of the flavour combinations below.

MAKES 10–12 POPSICLES

FLAVOUR VARIATIONS

Chai
Add 1 teaspoon of ground cinnamon, ½ teaspoon of ground cardamom, ½ teaspoon of ground cloves, 1 teaspoon of finely grated ginger and 1 tablespoon of licorice root powder before blending.

Chocolate
Add 2 tablespoons of cacao powder before blending.

Avocado
Add 1 chopped avocado before blending.

During a recent trip to Perth, I had the good fortune to meet Cat Cannizzaro, one of Australia's leading raw food gourmet chefs. Cat is renowned for her WildRaw handcrafted chocolate. If you're in Western Australia, I recommend you take one of Cat's hands-on chocolate classes to learn how to create her delicious treats for yourself. This cheesecake blew me away and Cat has kindly shared her recipe. It has a zesty freshness about it that will leave you feeling like you've had a treat without the heavy feeling that accompanies traditional high-sugar desserts. You will need to start this recipe the day before.

LEMON AND LIME CHEESECAKE

440 g cashews

coconut oil, for greasing

210 ml lemon juice

210 ml lime juice

1 teaspoon natural vanilla extract

½ teaspoon sea salt

350 g honey

1 teaspoon lemon zest

1 teaspoon lime zest

270 ml coconut oil, melted

zest of 2 limes, to garnish

lime segments, to garnish (see tip)

violets, to garnish

BASE

160 g almonds (activated if possible, see page 176)

90 g desiccated coconut

6 medjool dates, pitted

1½ tablespoons coconut oil, melted

pinch of sea salt or Himalayan salt

½ teaspoon natural vanilla extract

Soak the cashews for 4 hours and then give them a good rinse.

Grease the base and sides of a 20 cm springform cake tin with coconut oil and line with baking paper.

To make the base, process the almonds and coconut in a food processor until broken up to a nice crumb. Add the dates, coconut oil, salt and vanilla extract and pulse until the mixture just comes together. Press the mixture firmly and evenly into the base of the springform tin. Refrigerate for at least 1 hour, or until firm.

Process the cashews, lemon and lime juice, vanilla and salt in a food processor until thick and hard to mix. Give it a stir using a spatula, then add the honey and pulse to combine. Add the lemon and lime zest and pulse again to combine. Pour in the coconut oil and process until smooth and creamy. Pour the mixture over the base and remove air bubbles by tapping the tin on the table.

Place in the freezer for 2–4 hours, or until firm.

Remove the cheesecake from the tin while frozen and transfer to a serving platter. Place in the fridge to defrost for about 2 hours. When you are ready to serve, decorate with the lime zest, lime segments and violets.

SERVES 8–10

TIP

To segment a lime, first remove the zest and white pith. Use a small, sharp knife to cut alongside the membrane of one segment to the centre of the lime. Cut along the other side of the segment and you should be able to remove the segment. Repeat this process for the remaining segments.

I am lucky enough to have a wonderful cook as my partner who is as health-focused as me. I normally don't go for treats, but Nic's cacao and carob bites are irresistible. Just remember that cacao is a stimulant so I wouldn't recommend eating these before bed – they are best as a mid-morning or afternoon pick-me-up. You can also omit the cacao and double the carob if you have concerns about eating cacao.

CACAO AND CAROB BITES

250 ml coconut oil, melted

1 teaspoon dried chilli flakes, or to taste

3 drops peppermint oil, or to taste

3 tablespoons cacao powder*

3 tablespoons carob powder*

1 tablespoon maca powder* (optional)

2 tablespoons honey

1 teaspoon finely grated ginger

2 teaspoons cinnamon verum powder* or ground cinnamon

pinch of sea salt

* See Glossary

Line a 20 cm × 14 cm tray with plastic wrap.

Place all the ingredients in a mixing bowl and stir until well combined. Spread onto the prepared tray and place in the fridge for 2 hours, or until set. If you are in a hurry, pop it in the freezer and it will set even faster.

Once set, flip it out of the tray onto a chopping board and cut or break into bite-sized pieces.

You will need to keep these bites in the fridge, as they will melt at room temperature. They will keep for 2–3 weeks, but if your family is like mine, they won't last nearly that long!

MAKES ABOUT 300 G

VARIATION

For a fruit and nut version, omit the chilli flakes and peppermint oil and instead add 230 g of chopped nuts (brazil nuts, macadamia nuts, whatever you like) and 130 g of dried cranberries or blueberries (or a mixture of both).

I first had this drink in Indonesia on a surfing trip. I could not believe how good it tasted and I became totally addicted to it. The turmeric is the key to making this juice shine – just make sure you wear gloves when handling it, as it can stain your fingers and clothes. I like to add some fermented papaya juice or olive leaf probiotic drink for extra health benefits. These drinks are available from health food stores and some chemists, but don't worry if you can't find them – this drink will still be good for you and taste just as great.

LEMON, HONEY AND TURMERIC JUICE

2 lemons, peeled

1 large orange, peeled

3 cm piece of fresh turmeric, peeled

pinch of ground cloves

1 tablespoon manuka honey* (UMF16+ if possible)

2 tablespoons fermented papaya juice* or olive leaf probiotic drink (optional)

lemon or lime wedges, to serve (optional)

* *See Glossary*

Place the lemons, oranges and turmeric in a juicer and process. Pour 250 ml of filtered water through the juicer (to mix in with the juice).

Dissolve the ground cloves and honey in 2 tablespoons of warm water (make sure it isn't hot, as it will destroy the medicinal properties of the manuka honey). Stir the honey mixture and fermented papaya juice or olive leaf probiotic drink (if using) into the juice and serve with a wedge of fresh lime or lemon if desired.

SERVES 2

Lemon, honey and turmeric juice

Super juice (see recipe on page 232)

A quick way to get some goodness into your body is a fresh super juice. Feel free to play around with different vegetables, depending on the season, but remember to go easy on the fruit to ensure you don't send your GI levels sky-high.

SUPER JUICE

3 carrots

1 small bunch of kale (about 350 g), central stalks removed

150 g baby spinach

½ large beetroot

2 celery stalks

½ cucumber

2 green apples

1 orange, peeled

3 cm piece of ginger, peeled

Juice all the ingredients and serve immediately.

SERVES 2

Why do we need to have milk? It is a good question, and I do not for one minute believe that milk from a cow or goat or any other animal is good for us. So why the fascination with nut, soy, quinoa and rice milks? Well, we live in a culture that thinks cereal in the morning is part and parcel of our way of living. I probably have a bowl of cereal every couple of weeks. The rest of the time, it is meat, seafood or eggs and veggies for brekkie. When I do decide to chomp on some seeds and nuts, I use homemade nut milk, which is delicious and great in a cup of chai tea or a smoothie.

NUT MILK

1 cup activated almonds, cashews, walnuts, macadamias or other nuts (page 176)

1–1.2 litres water

Place the nuts in a blender with the water and blend for a couple of minutes. You can add more water for a thinner nut milk or less water if you want a thicker, creamier nut milk.

Line a bowl with a piece of muslin so that the muslin hangs over the edges. Pour the blended nuts and water into the bowl. Pick up the edges of the muslin and squeeze out all the milk.

Pour into a large jar or bottle, place in the fridge and give it a good shake when you want to use it. The nut milk will last for 3–4 days.

MAKES ABOUT 1.2 LITRES

TIPS

The leftover solids from nut milk can be added to smoothies or chia puddings (page 14) for an extra hit of protein and fibre. You can also spread the solids out on a lined baking tray and place in a 50°C oven for 3–4 hours, or until completely dried. Use this dried nut meal in mueslis, cookies or any baked goods that call for ground nuts. Store in an airtight container in the pantry for up to 3 months.

Kefir is a wonderful fermented beverage to make at home. The health benefits are outstanding: it can help restore the intestinal flora of people who are recovering from illness or who have taken a course of antibiotics. You can make it with water as the base, but I'm a sucker for young coconut water and love the addition of ginger. I think this is good enough to bottle.

COCONUT AND GINGER KEFIR

3 young coconuts*

1–2 probiotic capsules* or
1½ tablespoons water kefir grains*

1 tablespoon finely grated ginger

* *See Glossary*

You will need a 750 ml glass jar for this recipe. Wash it in hot soapy water, then run it through the dishwasher on a hot rinse cycle to sterilise. If you don't have a dishwasher, boil it in a large pot on the stove for 10 minutes, then put it on a tray in a 150°C oven to dry.

Open the coconuts by cutting a circular hole in the top of each one. Strain the coconut water into the sterilised jar and set aside to come to room temperature. If using a probiotic capsule, open the capsule and add the contents to the coconut water. If using water kefir grains, add them straight into the coconut water. Add the ginger and use a wooden spoon to stir well.

Cover the jar with a piece of muslin and a rubber band. Place in a dark spot at room temperature for 24–48 hours. Your kefir is ready when the water turns from relatively clear to cloudy white. To test it, pour some into a glass after 24–30 hours – do not taste directly from the bottle. It should taste sour, with no sweetness left, like coconut beer. If it still tastes a bit sweet, give it some more fermenting time. The kefir will last for up to 2 weeks in the fridge.

MAKES ABOUT 750 ML

TIPS

All materials that come into contact with the kefir need to be sterilised. You want to grow good bacteria, not bad, so boil or wash everything, including your hands.

Metal can react with kefir in a way that yields unhealthy elements in your final product. Stainless steel is the most inert metal, but it still reacts. Glass bottles are preferable to plastic since kefir actually breaks down plastic and you end up eating it. Limited contact is fine, but prolonged contact is not a good idea.

Only use coconut water from young coconuts – store-bought coconut water doesn't work because it is pasteurised.

Never add probiotics to refrigerated water as it will drastically slow the fermentation process.

Coconut and ginger
kefir

Nut milk (see recipe
on page 233)

Chocolate is such a treat in its raw, organic form – cacao. And this smoothie is a great way to get a chocolate fix without the nasty side effects that come with the sugar-filled, addictive packets that seem to be strategically placed at every checkout counter. If you are making this for your kids, you might want to use carob instead of cacao, as it doesn't contain any caffeine.

CHOCOLATE SMOOTHIE

2 tablespoons unsweetened cacao powder*

1 tablespoon maca powder*

1 tablespoon licorice root powder*

80 g blueberries (fresh or frozen)

1 ripe banana

500 ml coconut water*

125 ml coconut milk or coconut cream

25 g shredded coconut

10 almonds (activated if possible, see page 176)

10 macadamia nuts (activated if possible, see page 176)

1 tablespoon honey (optional)

* See Glossary

Combine all the ingredients in a blender and process until smooth and creamy. If you're using fresh blueberries instead of frozen, I suggest you add a little ice to the blender, too, so that your smoothie is nice and cold.

Pour into tall glasses and serve.

SERVES 2

Chocolate smoothie

Green and blue
smoothie
(see recipe
on page 239)

Kiddy yumyum
smoothie (see recipe
on page 238)

My girls love their smoothies, and they're a great way to encourage them to try a little spirulina. You can gradually up the amount of spirulina once your kids get used to the taste, but be ready to explain the reason why their smoothie is greener. I go with the Popeye story and let them know that it's a special ingredient, grown in water, that helps them become healthy, fast and strong – and next thing I know . . . it's down the hatch.

KIDDY YUMYUM SMOOTHIE

1 teaspoon spirulina*

160 g blueberries (fresh or frozen)

60 g raspberries (fresh or frozen)

1 ripe banana

125 ml coconut milk or coconut cream

125 ml coconut water*

25 g shredded coconut

1 tablespoon coconut oil

1 tablespoon licorice root powder*

10 almonds (activated if possible, see page 176)

* *See Glossary*

Combine all the ingredients in a blender and process until smooth and creamy. If you're using fresh berries, I suggest you add a little ice to the blender, too, if you want your smoothie to be cold.

Pour into glasses to serve.

SERVES 2–3 LITTLE TACKERS

Nic loves making smoothies, and this is one her best creations. When I'm in a rush to get out the door, I'll often whiz up one of these for breakfast. It is packed full of everything our bodies need to start the day: protein, omega-3s, B vitamins, antioxidants, fibre, probiotics and vitamin D3.

GREEN AND BLUE SMOOTHIE

10 macadamia nuts

10 almonds

750 ml coconut water* or water

160 g blueberries (fresh or frozen)

2 kiwifruit, peeled

1 tablespoon spirulina*

1 tablespoon maca powder*

1 tablespoon honey

1 tablespoon coconut oil

25 g shredded coconut

2 eggs

3 tablespoons Coconut and Ginger Kefir (page 234)

* *See Glossary*

Place the macadamia nuts and almonds in a bowl, cover with water and soak for at least 2 hours, or overnight. Drain and rinse.

Place the nuts in a blender with the rest of the ingredients and blend until smooth and creamy. If you're using fresh berries instead of frozen, you can add some ice to the blender to make sure your smoothie is cold.

Pour into glasses and serve.

SERVES 2

I'm not much of a dessert guy, but I love to sip on a big cup of this tea after dinner, or at any time of day for that matter. Cloves are one of the best antioxidants, and they don't cost a fortune. Ginger and licorice root are both wonderful digestive aids, making this cup of goodness an ideal after-dinner treat.

MY FAVOURITE TEA

1 teaspoon ground cinnamon

½ teaspoon ground cardamom

½ teaspoon ground cloves

1 teaspoon finely grated ginger

1 tablespoon licorice root powder*

1 teaspoon honey

coconut cream or coconut milk, to taste

* *See Glossary*

Bring 1 litre of water to the boil in a saucepan. Remove from the heat, add the cinnamon, cardamom, cloves, ginger, licorice root and honey and allow to steep for 5 minutes. Add the coconut cream or milk, stir and serve.

SERVES 2

GREEN JUICE

This juice is a fantastic way to get some extra greens into your diet. Play around with the ingredients if you like, but make sure you don't use too much fruit as your juice will be so high in natural sugars that it won't do you any favours. Stick to vegetables, herbs, ginger, lemon and lime, and if you need to sweeten it, use a bit of green apple as I have done here.

1 cucumber

½ bunch of kale (about 200 g)

4 celery sticks

3 Granny Smith apples

1 lemon, peeled

½ handful of mint or parsley leaves

5 cm piece of ginger

Juice all the ingredients and serve immediately.

SERVES 1–2

ORANGE, CARROT AND BEETROOT JUICE

I am a huge fan of vegetable juices – working with the seasons you can make the most beautiful, nutrient-rich drinks to help supplement your diet. If you don't like juicing because you're worried about missing out on the fibre, then try popping the ingredients into a high-speed blender instead. Just be careful, though, as this can be a bit full-on for people who have a gut flora imbalance and cannot handle too many raw vegetables. If this is you, stick with juicing because it is a lot gentler on the digestive system.

3 navel oranges, peeled

8 carrots

5 cm piece of ginger

2.5 cm piece of fresh turmeric

4 beetroot, roughly chopped

Juice all the ingredients and serve immediately.

SERVES 1–2

Orange, carrot and
beetroot juice

Green juice

CHERMOULA

1 large handful of coriander
leaves, chopped

1 large handful of flat-leaf parsley
leaves, chopped

1 large handful of mint leaves,
chopped

3 garlic cloves, chopped

2 teaspoons ground cumin

2 teaspoons ground coriander

1 teaspoon paprika

1 small red chilli, chopped

3 tablespoons lemon juice

125 ml olive oil

sea salt and freshly ground black
pepper

Mix the herbs, garlic, spices, chilli and lemon juice in a food processor.
While the motor is running, drizzle in the oil and process until smooth.
Season with salt and pepper. The chermoula will last for 3–4 days in
the fridge.

MAKES ABOUT 250 ML

GREEN TAHINI

270 g unhulled tahini*

170 ml lemon juice

2 teaspoons sea salt

freshly ground black pepper

2 very large handfuls of flat-leaf
parsley leaves

1 small handful of coriander leaves

3 garlic cloves, peeled

pinch of ground cumin (optional)

* *See Glossary*

Place all the ingredients in a food processor or blender with 250 ml of
water and process for a few minutes until thoroughly combined. Store in
the fridge for up to 5 days.

MAKES ABOUT 700 ML

Green tahini

Harissa (see recipe on page 248)

Chermoula

HARISSA

10 dried long red chillies

2 long red chillies

½ teaspoon caraway seeds

¼ teaspoon coriander seeds

¼ teaspoon cumin seeds

4 garlic cloves, chopped

80 ml olive oil

2 tablespoons lemon juice

½ teaspoon tomato paste

½ teaspoon sea salt

Preheat the oven to 200°C.

Place the dried chillies in a bowl and cover with hot water. Soak for 30 minutes, or until soft. Drain and set aside.

Place the long red chillies on a baking tray and roast for 20 minutes, or until lightly charred. Transfer to a brown paper bag or wrap in paper towel to cool. When cool, scrape away the charred skin and roughly chop.

Lightly toast the caraway, coriander and cumin seeds in a dry frying pan over medium heat for about 3 minutes, or until aromatic. Grind in a spice grinder or with a mortar and pestle.

Place the soaked dried chillies, roasted chillies, ground seeds and all the remaining ingredients in a food processor and pulse until well combined and smooth. Store in a glass jar in the fridge for up to 1 month.

MAKES ABOUT 250 ML

CAULIFLOWER RICE

1 head cauliflower, chopped

2 tablespoons coconut oil

sea salt and freshly ground black pepper

Place the cauliflower in a food processor and pulse into tiny, fine cauliflower pieces – it should resemble rice.

Add the coconut oil to a frying pan and place over medium heat. Lightly cook the cauliflower for 4–6 minutes, or until soft. Season with salt and pepper and serve.

SERVES 4

Tangy red chilli dressing

Green goddess dressing

GREEN GODDESS DRESSING

½ avocado

3 tablespoons coconut milk

3 tablespoons lemon juice

1 garlic clove, finely chopped

2 anchovy fillets, finely chopped

½ cup roughly chopped flat-leaf parsley leaves

3 tablespoons roughly chopped basil leaves

1 tablespoon roughly chopped tarragon leaves

¼ teaspoon sea salt

125 ml extra-virgin olive oil

Place all the ingredients except the olive oil in a food processor or blender and process until well combined.

With the motor running, slowly pour in the oil and process until the dressing thickens and the herbs are finely chopped. Store in the fridge for up to 5 days.

MAKES 250 ML

TANGY RED CHILLI DRESSING

2 tablespoons Korean chilli paste (gochujang)*

1 tablespoon apple cider vinegar*

1 teaspoon honey

2 teaspoons sesame oil

* See Glossary

Place all the ingredients in a bowl with 1 tablespoon of water and whisk until well combined. Store in the fridge for 2–3 days.

MAKES ABOUT 100 ML

FRIED GARLIC OR SHALLOTS

250 ml coconut oil

6 garlic cloves or 4 French shallots, thinly sliced

Melt the coconut oil in a small saucepan over medium heat. Add the garlic or shallots and cook for 2–3 minutes, or until golden. Remove with a slotted spoon and drain on paper towel.

The coconut oil will have taken on a lovely garlicky flavour and you can re-use it for sautéing vegetables or cooking meat, chicken or fish.

MAKES 4–5 TABLESPOONS

AÏOLI

4 egg yolks

2 teaspoons Dijon or Fermented Mustard (page 203)

2 tablespoons apple cider vinegar*

2 tablespoons lemon juice

6 Garlic Confit cloves (page 255), finely chopped

400 ml olive oil

sea salt and freshly ground black pepper

* See Glossary

Place the egg yolks, mustard, vinegar, lemon juice, garlic and some salt in a food processor or blender and process until combined. With the motor running, slowly pour in the oil in a thin stream and process until the aïoli is thick and creamy. Season with salt and pepper. Store in the fridge for 4–5 days.

MAKES ABOUT 500 ML

Fried shallots

Garlic confit
(see recipe on page 255)

Aïoli

Fried garlic

Coconut dressing

GARLIC CONFIT

150 g (about 25) garlic cloves, peeled

250 ml coconut oil

Place the garlic cloves and coconut oil in a saucepan over very low heat (you do not want the oil to boil). Cook for 2 hours, or until the garlic is beautifully soft. Transfer the garlic and oil to a sealed jar and store in the fridge for up to 3 months.

MAKES 150 G

COCONUT DRESSING

250 ml vegetable stock (for a recipe, see page 36), plus 50 g cooked vegetables from the stock

½ teaspoon sea salt

flesh of 4 young coconuts*

½ teaspoon pau d'arco powder*

1 teaspoon slippery elm powder*

freshly ground black pepper

* See Glossary

Place the stock and cooked vegetables in a food processor or blender and process until smooth. Add the salt, coconut flesh, pau d'arco powder and slippery elm powder and process again until smooth. Add pepper to taste. The dressing will last for 2–3 days in the fridge.

MAKES ABOUT 450 ML

GLOSSARY

APPLE CIDER VINEGAR

I use raw, organic apple cider vinegar, which is sometimes labelled 'apple cider vinegar with mother'. The mother is made of enzymes and bacteria and has a cobweb-like appearance. Apple cider vinegar is rich in potassium and is believed to help clear up skin conditions. I love using it in dressings and stocks (see page 34) and often dilute some in warm water to make a great morning drink. Raw apple cider vinegar can be found at health food stores.

BAHARAT

Baharat is a Middle Eastern spice blend that includes black pepper, coriander, paprika, cardamom, nutmeg, cumin, cloves and cinnamon. It is great for seasoning meats and vegetables, adding to dips and sauces, or using as a dry rub or marinade for veggies, meat and fish. Look for baharat at Middle Eastern grocers and delis.

BONITO FLAKES

Bonito flakes are made from the bonito fish, which is like a small tuna. The fish is smoked, fermented, dried and shaved, and the end product looks similar to wood shavings. Bonito flakes are used to garnish Japanese dishes, or in sauces such as ponzu, soups such as miso and in dashi (Japanese stock). You can find bonito flakes in Japanese and Asian grocers.

BROWN RICE SYRUP

Brown rice syrup is made from fermented cooked rice and is treated with enzymes from sprouted barley. It can be used to replace refined sugar in baking – 1 cup of sugar can be replaced with 1 cup of brown rice syrup. Brown rice syrup has a low glycaemic value, which means it does not cause an insulin spike like other sweeteners. It also contains vitamin B, thiamine, niacin, magnesium, zinc, vitamin B6 and vitamin K. Just make sure you read the label when purchasing it, as some syrups are made using genetically modified enzymes. You can find it at some supermarkets or at health food stores.

BUCKWHEAT

Buckwheat is the seed of a flowering fruit that is related to rhubarb and sorrel. It is gluten free and is a popular substitute for wheat. Buckwheat is high in protein, containing all nine essential amino acids, including lysine. It is also rich in iron, antioxidants, magnesium, zinc, copper and niacin. Try adding buckwheat to salads or using it instead of rice or porridge. You can also buy buckwheat in flour form, which is great for gluten-free baking. Look for buckwheat in health food stores and some supermarkets.

CACAO AND CAROB POWDERS

Cacao powder comes from cacao beans that are fermented, dried, peeled and then cold pressed to extract about 75 percent of the cacao butter, leaving a dark brown paste. After drying, the remaining cacao solids are processed to make fine, unsweetened cacao powder.

Cacao powder is incredibly rich in antioxidants and also contains zinc, calcium, iron, copper, sulphur and potassium. Carob powder is made from the pod of the carob tree and is a great substitute for cacao if you want to avoid caffeine. You can add cacao or carob powder to your smoothies, tea, coffee, protein drinks, desserts or anything else you can think of. I choose raw, organic cacao and carob powders and these can be found at health food stores.

CHIA SEEDS

Chia seeds come from a Latin American plant and they pack a huge punch when it comes to nutrients. They are an excellent source of protein and also contain omega-3 and omega-6 fatty acids, calcium, potassium, iron and magnesium. When placed in liquid, chia seeds swell to 17 times their original size, so they are a great substitute for traditional thickening agents like cornstarch. I love sprinkling chia seeds into smoothies, muesli, salads and desserts. You can buy them from health food stores and some supermarkets.

CINNAMON VERUM POWDER

Cinnamon verum is made from the inner bark of a Sri Lankan tree and is also known as 'true cinnamon'. It has a more subtle and slightly sweeter flavour than other kinds of cinnamon. Some studies have shown that cinnamon verum may have the potential to help regulate blood-sugar levels. You can add cinnamon verum powder to desserts and smoothies as well as curries. It is available at health food stores, but if you can't find any, regular cinnamon (made from cassia bark) can be substituted.

COCONUT VINEGAR

Raw coconut vinegar is made from the sap of the coconut tree, which is rich in phosphorus, potassium, iron, magnesium and other minerals. It is quite cloudy and has a pungent, yeasty flavour. It is great in dressings, sauces and curries. You can buy coconut vinegar from health food stores.

COCONUT WATER

Coconut water is the watery, white liquid found inside young coconuts. It is rich in amino acids, enzymes, dietary fibre, vitamin C and minerals such as potassium, magnesium and manganese, while also being low in cholesterol and chlorides. Coconut water is great for smoothies, drinks, ice cream or even drinking on its own on a summer's day. You will find coconut water at health food stores and some supermarkets – make sure you check the label carefully as some brands contain added sugar.

CURRY LEAVES

The curry tree is native to India and Sri Lanka and its leaves are used widely in the cuisines of these countries. They are very aromatic and are often added to curries, soups and snacks. It is best to source fresh curry leaves if possible – from Asian supermarkets or some specialty greengrocers – as they will lend a much stronger aroma and flavour to your dish.

DAIKON

Daikon, or Japanese radish, is a large, white radish that is commonly used in Japanese, Korean and South-East Asian cuisines. It has a wide variety of uses – it is pickled, grated into sauces, simmered in broths and even stir-fried. Daikon is low in calories and contains high levels of vitamin C. It can be found at Asian supermarkets and some regular supermarkets.

DANDELION LEAVES

Dandelion leaves are long, dark green, strongly indented leaves with a bitter, peppery taste. They contain high levels of vitamin A and potassium. The leaves are often consumed as a nutritious salad green during spring and summer. Dandelion leaves can be found at specialty greengrocers.

DRIED CHESTNUTS

Dried chestnuts are chestnuts that have been roasted, peeled and dehydrated. They can be found at Asian supermarkets and are great for soups, casseroles, stuffings and salads. If you'd like to make your own dried chestnuts, cut a large 'X' into the flat side of your chestnuts with a sharp paring knife all the way through the skin. Place the chestnuts on a baking tray and roast in a 180°C oven for 12–15 minutes, depending on the size of the nuts. Remove from the oven and peel as soon as they are cool enough to handle. (Once they are completely cool they are difficult to peel.) Cut the chestnuts in half and place on a wire rack in a 125°C oven for up to 10 hours, or until completely dry. Cool, then store in an airtight container for up 12 months.

DULSE FLAKES

Dulse flakes are made from a red algae that grows on the northern coasts of the Atlantic and Pacific oceans. It is rich in protein and a good source of many vitamins and minerals, including iodine. I like sprinkling some dulse flakes into nori rolls (page 91) and they are also great in dressings or added to salads and soups. Look for dulse flakes at health food stores or online.

EGGS

The best eggs come from free-range chickens, which are allowed to roam freely outside in the sunshine, eat insects and plants, and have a far healthier and happier life than ones trapped in cages. Free-range eggs taste better, have stronger shells, are less runny, and have firmer and brighter yolks. They also contain less cholesterol and saturated fat than caged eggs, and have higher levels of vitamin A, E and D, protein, beta-carotene and omega-3 fatty acids. I use extra-large eggs in my recipes.

FERMENTED PAPAYA JUICE

Fermented papaya juice is a potent antioxidant and is also believed to have antibacterial and immune-boosting properties. It is fantastic added to any kind of juice or smoothie and can be found at health food stores and online.

FISH SAUCE

Fish sauce is liquid extracted from the fermentation of fish with sea salt. It is used as a condiment or seasoning in Vietnam, Thailand, Cambodia, Japan and many other Asian countries. Fish sauce is great for making dipping sauces, and is also used in marinades, stir-fries, curries, soups and dressings. When choosing your fish sauce, make sure you check the label as many brands have unnecessary sugar added. Try to find one of the premium brands that are made traditionally, using only fermented fish and water. You can find fish sauce in supermarkets or Asian grocers.

GALANGAL

Galangal is similar in appearance to ginger and has been used in Thai cooking for more than a thousand years. It is available in Asian supermarkets and some regular supermarkets, and is believed to relieve indigestion, flatulence, nausea and hiccups. It is fantastic in many kinds of Asian dishes, especially curries such as Burmese Beef Cheek Curry (page 171).

GELATINE

I always choose gelatine that has come from organic, grass-fed beef. Vegetarian substitutes for gelatine include agar agar and carrageen, which are made from two different types of seaweed. Sometimes these aren't as strong as regular gelatine, so you may need to increase the quantity. Some kosher gelatines are also vegan. You can buy gelatine made from organic, grass-fed beef, agar agar and carrageen from health food stores or online.

GINSENG ROOT

Ginseng root is found in eastern Asia (mostly Korea and north-eastern China) and North America. The plant has beautifully shaped green leaves and bright red berries, however, it is only the root that has any medicinal value. Ginseng is believed to improve mood and memory, boost endurance, reduce fatigue, bolster immunity, balance metabolism, prevent headaches and many other things. Ginseng root can be used in soups (see Korean Ginseng, Chicken and Buckwheat Soup on page 50), and is also great to infuse in teas. It can be found at Asian supermarkets and some greengrocers.

GOJI BERRIES

Goji berries are mainly grown in China, Mongolia and Tibet. They are bright pink and have a mild, tangy taste that is slightly sweet and sour. Goji berries are usually sold in dried form and have the same kind of shape and chewy texture as raisins. They contain all the essential amino acids and have the highest concentration of protein of any fruit. They are also loaded with vitamin C, carotenoids, fibre, iron, calcium, zinc, selenium and many other important trace minerals. Goji berries are great for adding to mueslis, desserts, sweet sauces and puddings. Goji berry powder is also available and can be stirred directly into juices, herbal teas, coconut water or even water. Goji berries can be found at your local supermarket or health food store.

HONEY AND MAPLE SYRUP

I rarely use sweeteners in my cooking, but when I do I usually opt for honey or maple syrup. I always choose raw, organic honey as it tastes better, is unprocessed and is produced in rural areas where there is much less pollution. Make sure that you choose a 100% pure maple syrup (made from boiling down the sap of maple trees) rather than imitation maple-flavoured syrup.

HORSERADISH

Horseradish has a penetrating smell and a very strong, hot, sharp taste. It is richer in vitamin C than orange or lemon, and is also a stimulant, diuretic and antiseptic. It is great with seafood and meat dishes. Horseradish can be bought fresh from your greengrocer, or as a puree in jars from the supermarket.

HULLED MILLET

Hulled millet is a gluten-free grain that is easily digestible and a great substitute for wheat and couscous. It has a mild flavour and can be added to soups and salads, or used to make porridge and flatbreads. Millet is a good source of B vitamins. It can be found at health food stores and some supermarkets.

JUNIPER BERRIES

Despite their name, juniper berries are actually cones rather than berries. They are purple in colour and are most famous for lending their flavour to gin. Juniper berries are fabulous with meat dishes and sauerkrauts or other fermented vegetable dishes (see pages 197–209). You can buy fresh or dried juniper berries from some health food stores, specialty food stores or online.

KAFFIR LIME LEAVES

Kaffir lime leaves have a mysterious smell unlike any other citrus. The leaves give a wholesome, lemony essence to your dishes and are fabulous for flavouring curry pastes. Kaffir lime leaves can be found at Asian supermarkets.

KELP NOODLES

Kelp noodles are clear noodles made from kelp seaweed. They contain more than 70 nutrients and minerals, including iodine, potassium, magnesium, calcium, iron and more than 21 amino acids. Kelp noodles are great for stir-fries, casseroles, soups and salads. You can find them at heath food stores.

KOREAN CHILLI PASTE (GOCHUJANG)

Korean chilli paste is made from glutinous rice powder mixed with fermented soybeans and red chilli peppers. It is used in Korean dishes such as Beef Bibimbap (page 169), salads, stir-fries, dips, stews, soups and marinated meat dishes. You can buy Korean chilli paste from Asian supermarkets and some regular supermarkets.

KOREAN CHILLI POWDER (GOCHUGARU)

Korean chilli powder is made from thin red chillies that are dried in the sun and ground. It has smoky, fruity sweet notes, with a hot kick, and is used to make classic Korean dishes such as kimchi (for a recipe, see page 208) and bulgogi. It is also great for stir-fries, dipping sauces and meat marinades. You can find Korean chilli powder in Asian supermarkets.

LICORICE ROOT POWDER

When ground into a powder, licorice root has a slightly sweet flavour and can be added to smoothies, drinks and desserts. Licorice root has been used in Chinese medicine for many years and is believed to help with a wide range of conditions, including digestive problems. Licorice root powder can be found at health food stores.

MACA POWDER

Maca is a rainforest herb that is high in protein and other nutrients. It is believed to increase energy and support the immune system. Try adding a spoonful of maca powder to your smoothies for a protein boost. Or, for a treat, try some Date, Chia and Maca Balls (page 182).

MANUKA HONEY

Manuka honey is sourced from forests in New Zealand where the bees collect pollen primarily from the manuka plant. The honey has antibacterial properties and can be used to treat minor wounds and bites. It has a strong, earthy flavour and can be added to smoothies, drizzled over your muesli or dessert, or used in any way that regular honey is. Manuka honey can be found at health food stores and pharmacies. Try to buy one with a high UMF (Unique Manuka Factor) rating – the higher the rating, the stronger its antibacterial qualities.

MISO PASTE

Miso paste is made from fermented soybeans. It has a salty taste, buttery texture and unique nutritional profile that make it a versatile condiment for a host of different recipes (see Grilled Fish with Miso on page 116), and a foundation for traditional miso soup. In addition to soybeans, miso paste can include rice, barley or wheat. Miso paste ranges in colour from white to brown – the darker the colouring, the more robust the flavour and saltiness.

NORI SHEETS

Nori is a dark green, paper-like, toasted seaweed used for most kinds of sushi and other Japanese dishes. Nori provides an abundance of essential nutrients and is rich in vitamins, iron, minerals, amino acids, omega-3 and omega-6, and anti-oxidants. Nori sheets are commonly used to roll sushi, but they can also be added to salads, soups, and fish, meat and vegetable dishes. You can buy nori sheets from Asian grocers and most supermarkets.

OKRA

Also known as ladyfingers, okra is and are popular in many cuisines, including Indian, Israeli, Japanese and Mediterranean. It is best used when very young, while the pod is green, tender and immature. Okra is a good source of vitamin A and C, fibre, calcium and iron. It has a glutinous texture when cooked and brings body to soups, stews and curries (such as Sour Sardine Curry on page 115).

PANDAN LEAVES

The long, green leaves of the tropical pandan plant are used to flavour many different dishes in South-East Asia. In Thailand pandan leaves are often used in desserts and drinks, as well as to wrap savoury chicken parcels. Pieces of pandan leaf can be added to rice dishes or curries to lend a delicate aroma. Pandan is available in leaf or paste form at Asian supermarkets.

PAU D'ARCO POWDER

Pau d'arco powder is made from the dried bark of the South American pau d'arco tree. It adds a unique flavour to dishes, is high in antioxidants and is said to boost immune function and help treat fungal infections. You can buy pau d'arco powder from health food stores.

PEPPER LEAVES

The heart-shaped leaves from the pepper (or pepper) plant are used in various cuisines throughout Asia. They are often added stir-fries and soups, or used to wrap parcels of food. They have a slightly bitter, peppery flavour and are believed by some to help with headaches and anxiety. You can find pepper leaves at Asian supermarkets.

POMEGRANATE MOLASSES

Pomegranate molasses is a beautifully thick, tangy and glossy reduction of pomegranate juice that has a sweet and sour flavour and is rich in antioxidants. Pomegranate molasses is used in Middle Eastern countries for glazing meat and chicken before roasting, and in sauces, salad dressings and marinades. Pomegranate molasses is available from Middle Eastern grocers and some delis.

PROBIOTIC CAPSULES

Probiotic capsules contain live bacteria that help to regulate digestion, clear up yeast infections and assist with conditions such as irritable bowel syndrome. These capsules need to be kept in the fridge. They can be swallowed whole, or opened up and used to ferment drinks such as kefir (page 234). Probiotic capsules can be found at pharmacies and health food stores.

QUINOA

Quinoa is a South American crop and is actually a seed rather than a grain. It is gluten free and contains high levels of protein, as well as some calcium, phosphorus and iron. Quinoa is available in many different varieties – white, red and black are the most common – and each one has a subtly different flavour. It is also available as flakes and flour. Quinoa is a fantastic substitute for rice and can also be used in salads or to make breakfast dishes such as porridge. You can find it at most supermarkets and health food stores.

RED DATES (JUJUBE)

Red dates are high in vitamins A, B1, B2 and C, protein, calcium, phosphorous, iron and magnesium. Red dates can be used in soups, salads, desserts, breakfast cereals, stir-fries and as a sweet to finish a meal. You can buy them from some Asian grocers, heath food stores and online.

SALT

I like to use sea salt or Himalayan salt in my cooking, as they are less processed than table salt, contain more minerals and have a lovely crunchy texture. Himalayan salt is light pink in colour due to the presence of a number of different minerals, including iron, magnesium, calcium and copper. You can purchase both sea salt and Himalayan salt at supermarkets and health food stores.

SHAOXING RICE WINE

Originating from the Chinese region of Shaoxing, this fermented rice wine is used widely for both drinking and cooking in China. Its flavour is similar to dry sherry and it can be added to marinades, soups, stocks and stir-fries. You'll find shaoxing rice wine in Asian supermarkets and some regular supermarkets.

SHISO LEAVES

Shiso leaves, also known as perilla, are commonly used in Japanese cuisine. There are red, purple and green varieties of shiso leaf and they are used in many ways – finely sliced on top of noodle dishes, chopped and added to batters, in tempura, or scattered over any number of dishes as a garnish. Shiso has quite a pungent, grassy flavour that is lost when it is cooked for a long time. You can find shiso leaves at Asian grocers.

SHRIMP PASTE (BELACAN)

Shrimp paste is used in many different Asian cuisines and is an essential ingredient in numerous curries and sauces. It is made from tiny shrimp mixed with salt and fermented, then ground into a smooth paste and sun dried. Shrimp paste has quite a powerful smell and taste, so should only be used in small quantities. You can find it in Asian grocers and some supermarkets.

SICHUAN PEPPERCORNS

Sichuan peppercorns have quite a different flavour to regular black peppercorns. They have lemony overtones and leave the tongue feeling tingly. They are used widely in spicy Sichuan cuisine, particularly in hot pots, stir-fries, noodle dishes and spice mixes. You will find Sichuan peppercorns at Asian supermarkets and some regular supermarkets.

SLIPPERY ELM POWDER

Slippery elm powder comes from the inner bark of the slippery elm tree. It is believed to help the digestive system and may assist in soothing an unsettled stomach. Some people also take slippery elm to help with coughs and skin problems. Slippery elm doesn't have a particularly strong flavour, so it can be added to smoothies, juices or sauces. You can buy it from heath food stores and pharmacies.

SPIRULINA

Spirulina is a microscopic blue-green algae. It's very high in protein and contains many vitamins and minerals, including vitamins A and B, and iron. Spirulina is believed to be good for your teeth, hair, skin and immune system. It is usually sold in powdered form and is great to use in smoothies, shakes, muesli, juices, drinks and desserts. You can buy spirulina from heath food stores and some supermarkets.

SUMAC

Sumac is a spice made from red sumac berries that have been dried and crushed. It has antimicrobial properties and a tangy, lemony flavour, which makes it ideal for pairing with seafood. It's also delicious in salad dressings.

TAHINI

Tahini is a paste made from ground sesame seeds and has a smooth, creamy texture. It is an excellent source of protein, copper and manganese and a good source of calcium, magnesium, iron, phosphorus, vitamin B1, zinc, selenium and essential fatty acids. Tahini is a well-known ingredient in North African, Greek, Turkish, and Middle Eastern cuisine. It is used to make hummus, dips and salad dressings. I prefer unhulled tahini, but there are also hulled varieties available, as well as black tahini made from black sesame seeds. You can find tahini in supermarkets and heath food stores.

TAMARI

Tamari is made with whole, fermented soybeans. It is similar to soy sauce, but is richer and less salty and has no wheat, so is gluten free. Tamari is mostly used in Asian cuisines and is perfect for stir-fries, marinades, dressings, soups and dipping sauces. You can find it in supermarkets or Asian grocers.

TAMARIND

Tamarind juice or pulp is made from the pods of the tamarind tree and is used as a souring agent, particularly in Indian dishes, chutneys and curries. It is also used to flavour pulse or rice dishes, or as an ingredient in sauces and side dishes for pork, chicken and fish. Tamarind has a mild laxative effect. It can be found at Asian grocers and some supermarkets.

TEMPEH

One of Indonesia's most famous foods, tempeh is similar to tofu but is made from whole, fermented soy beans rather than soy milk. It has more protein, fibre and vitamins than tofu and is easier to digest because of the fermentation. Tempeh is usually marinated and fried before being added to rice dishes, stir-fries, salads and stews. Its firm texture and earthy flavour make it a great substitute for meat. Look for tempeh at Asian supermarkets and some regular supermarkets.

TRUFFLE OIL

Truffle oil is made by infusing olive oil with white or black truffles. It has a beautiful, intense aroma and amazing flavour. Truffle oil is for finishing dishes rather than for cooking with. It is great added to dressings, or drizzled over risottos, soups and salads. Only use a small amount as it can be quite powerful in flavour. You can buy truffle oil from delis, gourmet stores or online.

VEGETABLE STARTER CULTURE

A vegetable starter culture is a preparation used to kick-start the fermentation process when culturing vegetables (see pages 197–209). I prefer to use a broad-spectrum starter sourced from organic vegetables rather than one grown from dairy, as this ensures your fermented product will contain the highest number of living, active bacteria and will produce consistently successful results free of pathogens. Vegetable starter culture usually comes in sachets and can be purchased at health food stores or online.

WAKAME

Wakame is an edible seaweed commonly used in Japanese, Korean and Chinese cuisine. It is great in soups, salads and stir-fries. Wakame contains iron, magnesium, iodine, calcium and lignans. You can find it in Asian grocers and some supermarkets.

WASABI

Also known as Japanese horseradish, this spicy paste is made from the roots of the wasabi plant. It is delicious with Japanese dishes such as sushi, sashimi and soba noodles, and is also a powerful antioxidant that supports natural liver and digestive detoxification. You can buy it from Asian grocers and most supermarkets.

WATER KEFIR GRAINS

Water kefir grains, also known as tibicos, sugar kefir grains or Japanese water crystals, are used to make fermented drinks. These grains feed off sugar to produce lactic acid, acetic acid, various other acids and carbon dioxide gas, which carbonates the drink. Water kefir grains can be cultured in a solution of sugar and water, but I like to use young coconut water. Drinks made from water kefir grains can help to balance the bacteria in your stomach, aiding digestion and fighting off harmful bacteria. You can purchase water kefir grains at health food stores or online.

WATER SPINACH

Also known as Chinese watercress, water spinach has high levels of protein, calcium, iron, potassium and vitamins A, B and C. Water spinach can be used in almost anything, including stir-fries, quiches, omelettes, soups, fillings, casseroles and curries. You can find water spinach in Asian grocers and some fruit and vegetable markets.

YOUNG COCONUTS

Young coconuts are harvested at around 5–7 months and are usually white in colour. The best way to open one is to cut a circle in the top using a large knife and then prise this circle off. The amount of coconut water inside varies but is usually around 250 ml. It is a good source of potassium and makes a refreshing drink on a hot day. Once you've poured the water out of the coconut, you can scoop the soft flesh out using a spoon. The flesh can be used to make ice cream (page 220), chia seed puddings (page 14) and many other delicious treats. Look for young coconuts at Asian supermarkets and health food stores.

YUZU JUICE

Yuzu is a Japanese citrus fruit that has an extraordinary spicy citrus flavour, somewhere between a lemon and a lime. Yuzu juice is very high in vitamin C and is great in cocktails, dressings, dips and sashimi dishes. You can buy yuzu juice from Asian grocers.

ZA'ATAR

Za'atar is a Middle Eastern spice mix that is used to flavour meats, seafood, eggs, soups, vegetables and poultry. Za'atar contains thyme, sumac, sesame seeds, oregano, marjoram and salt. You can buy it from Middle Eastern grocers, delis and some supermarkets.

THANK YOU

This book wouldn't have been possible without Nicola Robinson entering my life when she did. Thank you, Angel, for your love, support, wisdom and belief in me to be the best I can be. I love you!

To my darling little 'bunnies', Chilli and Indii. You girls grow wiser and more beautiful every day and I look forward to seeing where the journey of life takes you. I am sure you will enrich so many lives.

To Mary Small, thank you for enabling me to create the book that I had in my mind exactly as I wanted it, without dumbing it down or taking away the message that I wanted to express.

Mark Roper, you are a magician behind the lens. Thank you for the wonderful images – they really make the food jump off the page.

Deb Kaloper, the queen of styling, you definitely have a rare and special talent for making food look relaxed and accessible.

Megan Johnston, thank you for your careful and thorough editing.

Kirby Armstrong, thank you for creating such a beautiful design for the book.

Thanks to Steve Brown and Kristine Duran-Thiessen for doing an excellent job of photographing and styling the cover and chapter openers.

Jane Winning, thank you for testing and correcting my recipes and words with your unwavering attention to detail.

The wonder twins, Monica and Jacinta, you have evolved and grown as chefs and I am proud to have you both give up your time to help me out on this project.

Thank you to my mentors, Nora Gedgaudas, Rudolph Elkhardt, Pete Bablis, William Davis, Pete Melov, Bruce Fife, David Gillespie, Loren Cordain, Sandor Katz, Donna Gates, Sally Fallon, Weston A Price, Mark Sisson, Rob Wolf, Joshua Rosenthal, Dr Natasha Campbell-McBride and Kitsa Yanniotis, as well as all of the other passionate people who dedicate their lives to helping others.

And lastly, thank you to my mum, Joy. I love you!

INDEX

First published as *Healthy Every Day* in 2014 by Macmillan Australia

This edition first published in the UK in 2015 by Macmillan
an imprint of Pan Macmillan, a division of Macmillan Publishers Limited
Pan Macmillan, 20 New Wharf Road, London N1 9RR
Basingstoke and Oxford
Associated companies throughout the world
www.panmacmillan.com

ISBN 978-1-4472-8748-3

Design and illustrations by Kirby Armstrong
Photography by Mark Roper
Prop and food styling by Deb Kaloper
Cover and chapter opener photography by Steve Brown
Cover and chapter opener styling by Kristine Duran-Thiessen
Food preparation by Monica Cannataci and Jacinta Cannataci
Edited by Megan Johnston
Typeset by Pauline Haas
Index by Jo Rudd
Colour reproduction by Splitting Image Colour Studio

The publisher would like to thank the following for their generosity
in providing props for the book: Anchor Ceramics, Craft Victoria,
Made in Japan, Tara Shackell Ceramics and American Apparel.

9 8 7 6 5 4 3 2

A CIP catalogue record for this book is available from
the British Library.

Printed in China by Wing King Tong

Visit **www.panmacmillan.com** to read more about all our books and
to buy them. You will also find features, author interviews and news of
any author events, and you can sign up for e-newsletters so that you're
always first to hear about our new releases.

A note on oven temperatures
All oven temperatures have been given in Celsius. For
gas equivalents, please use the conversion table below:

Celsius	Gas
110°C	gas ¼
120°C	gas ½
140°C	gas 1
150°C	gas 2
160°C	gas 3
180°C	gas 4
190°C	gas 5
200°C	gas 6
220°C	gas 7
230°C	gas 8
260°C	highest setting